THE GREAT WESTERN CANADA BUCKET LIST

ROBIN ESROCK

ONE -OF-A- KIND **TRAVEL EXPERIENCES**

DUNDURN

TORONTO

For my grandmother, Fanny Esrock

Library and Archives Canada Cataloguing in Publication
Esrock, Robin, 1974-, author

The great western Canada bucket list : one-of-a-kind travel experiences / Robin Esrock.

Issued in print and electronic formats.
ISBN 978-1-4597-2965-0 (pbk.).--ISBN 978-1-4597-2966-7 (pdf).--
ISBN 978-1-4597-2967-4 (epub)

1. Alberta--Guidebooks. 2. British Columbia--Guidebooks. 3. Esrock, Robin, 1974- --Travel--Alberta. 4. Esrock, Robin, 1974- -- Travel--British Columbia. 5. Alberta--Description and travel. 6. British Columbia--Description and travel. I. Title.

FC3657.E86 2015   917.12304'4   C2014-907093-4
C2014-907094-2

Editor: Allison Hirst
Cover and text concept: Tania Craan
Cover design: Courtney Horner
Text design: Laura Boyle
Cover images: T.J. Watt/ Robin Esrock/ Melissa Barnes, Penticton & Wine Country Tourism/ Joe Kalmek/ Paul Zizka, SkiBig3/ Robin Esrock/ Jeff Topham/ Ian Mackenzie (back)

1 2 3 4 5   19 18 17 16 15

Conseil des Arts du Canada   Canada Council for the Arts

Canada

ONTARIO ARTS COUNCIL
CONSEIL DES ARTS DE L'ONTARIO
an Ontario government agency
un organisme du gouvernement de l'Ontario

We acknowledge the support of the **Canada Council for the Arts** and the **Ontario Arts Council** for our publishing program. We also acknowledge the financial support of the **Government of Canada** through the **Canada Book Fund** and **Livres Canada Books**, and the **Government of Ontario** through the **Ontario Book Publishing Tax Credit** and the **Ontario Media Development Corporation**.

Care has been taken to trace the ownership of copyright material used in this book. The author and the publisher welcome any information enabling them to rectify any references or credits in subsequent editions.

J. Kirk Howard, President

The publisher is not responsible for websites or their content unless they are owned by the publisher.

Printed and bound in Canada.

Visit us at
Dundurn.com | @dundurnpress | Facebook.com/dundurnpress | Pinterest.com/dundurnpress

Dundurn
3 Church Street, Suite 500
Toronto, Ontario, Canada
M5E 1M2

CONTENTS

INTRODUCTION

"I thought I lived in God's Country, and then I came here," an Australian tourist tells me about his vacation in western Canada. We are descending in a carriage on the Sea to Sky Gondola, the latest attraction in a region full of them, with the green waters of the Howe Sound glittering below in the late afternoon sun.

Whatever your relationship with God, we can all understand the Aussie's sentiment. God's Country: a place of such incredible beauty that it belongs in a higher realm.

Having spent ten years travelling to six continents, I've found God's Country to have transparent, unlimited borders. Deserts offer a rare beauty. You can drink jungle air like an elixir, hang dreams on the fronds of beach palms, and breathe tranquility on the tundra. Yet I've also discovered that deep-cut fjords, dense coastal rainforests, soaring snow-tipped mountain peaks, and turquoise glacial lakes form the very foundation of what many conceive to be natural beauty. This beauty sits as the foundation of British Columbia and Alberta's bucket list — and we're just getting started.

You have to experience this before you die: It's a bold statement for any destination or activity. After all, we all have different tastes and interests, and when it comes to travel, just about anything can float your dinghy. A travel writer's job is to uncover the remarkable and the unique. Much like an accountant crunches spreadsheets, travel writers chase experiences. In doing so, we inspire ourselves, and our readers, too.

Several years ago, the topic of my column in the Canada Day issue of the *Globe and Mail* was "The Great Canadian Bucket List." I listed a dozen must-do experiences across the country. A publisher asked me if I was interested in turning that into a guidebook. But I've long felt traditional guidebooks can be as dry as a moon rock, which is why I've seldom used one in my journeys to more than

one hundred countries. Simply put: straight facts don't inspire juicy dreams. A ranch vacation in the Porcupine Hills, tracking the spirit bear, sailing in the Galapagos of the North — what does this even mean, and what does it feel like? If I hoped to write about the best of Canada, I was determined to experience the best of Canada. Thus began my two-year journey to every province and territory.

Years of international adventure taught me that meaningful travel is as much about the people you meet as the places you go. If I wanted to find compelling stories, I'd need to find the characters that don't live on Wikipedia. My *Great Canadian Bucket List* became a smash bestseller because one of those characters was an immigrant, discovering his new country with a sense of awe and wonder. And that happened to be me.

Like many tourists, my first impressions of coastal British Columbia left me speechless. I'd landed in Vancouver as an immigrant, without having ever stepped foot in North America. It was a bright August day, with fireworks scheduled that evening in English Bay. A day later, a friend took me on a ferry to the Gulf Islands. I'd seen similar scenery backpacking in Scandinavia, but not as *big*, and certainly not as accessible. When I discovered the Rocky Mountains, my visits to the Alps and Andes paled in comparison. Yes, you'll find elements of western Canada's beauty elsewhere, but not on this scale, and certainly not with the region's world-class hotel, dining, transportation, and attractions infrastructure. western Canada makes it exceptionally easy to tick off your bucket list, and to inspire new dreams.

Beyond the natural assets, I sought one-of-a-kind experiences unique to the region: snorkelling with tens of thousands of salmon, heli-yoga atop a mountaintop, digging for dinosaur fossils, and skiing inside a UNESCO World Heritage Site are just some of the adventures you'll find in these pages. Since I'd like nothing more than for you to follow in my footsteps, each chapter points to a companion website where you'll find practical information, videos, galleries, reading guides, and other bonus content.

Some of these Western Canada Bucket List experiences can cost a fortune; others are as free as a walk in Stanley Park. There's adventure, food, culture, history — hopefully something for everyone. My goal is to inform, inspire, and entertain both local readers and visitors with a personal journey into Canada's crown jewel. In truth, the scenery and attractions of British Columbia and Alberta sell themselves, but the context, insider tips, stories, and characters need a little nudge. It's been quite the adventure to get it onto these pages, into your hands, and inside your imagination. God's Country is indeed waiting, and so is your own bucket list.

Robin Esrock
Vancouver, B.C.

A Note: Western Canada often refers to the provinces of British Columbia, Alberta, Saskatchewan, and Manitoba. Since Manitoba and Saskatchewan will feature in their own Prairie edition, this book refers only to British Columbia and Alberta.

USING THIS BOOK

You will notice this book includes little information about prices, where to stay, where to eat, the best time to go, or what you should pack. Important stuff certainly, but practicalities that shift and change with far more regularity than print editions of a book. With this in mind, I've created online and social media channels to accompany the inspirational guide you hold in your hands. Here you will find all the information noted above, along with videos, galleries, reading guides, and more.

By visiting www.canadianbucketlist.com, you can also join our community of bucket listers, find exclusive discounts for many of the activities discussed in this book, win prizes, and debate the merits of these and other adventures. When you register, unlock the entire site by entering the code BUCK3TL15T, or access each item individually with the START HERE link at the end of each chapter.

DISCLAIMER

Tourism is a constantly changing business. Hotels may change names, restaurants may change owners, and some activities may no longer be available at all. Records fall and facts shift. While the utmost care has been taken to ensure the information provided is accurate, the author and publisher take no responsibility for errors, or for any incidents that might occur in your pursuit of these activities.

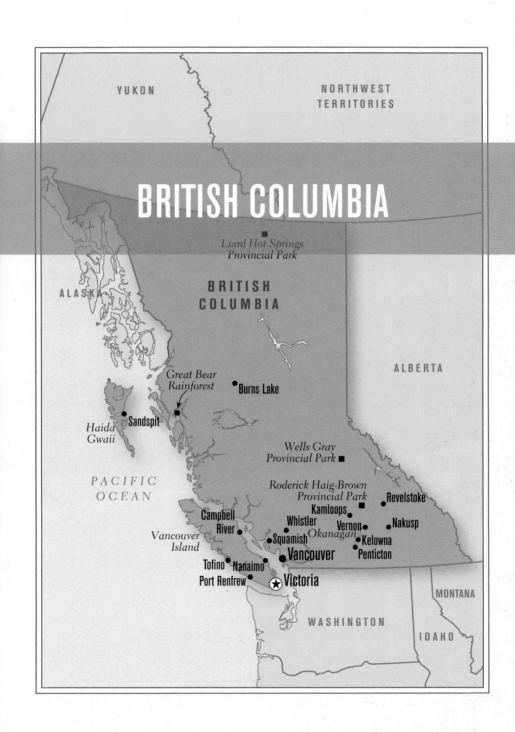

BRITISH COLUMBIA

YUKON

NORTHWEST TERRITORIES

Liard Hot Springs
Provincial Park

BRITISH
COLUMBIA

ALASKA

ALBERTA

Great Bear
Rainforest

Burns Lake

Haida
Gwaii

Sandspit

Wells Gray
Provincial Park

PACIFIC
OCEAN

Roderick Haig-Brown
Provincial Park

Revelstoke

Kamloops

Campbell
River

Whistler

Nakusp

Vernon

Vancouver
Island

Squamish

Okanagan

Kelowna

Penticton

Tofino

Nanaimo

Vancouver

Port Renfrew

Victoria

MONTANA

WASHINGTON

IDAHO

SAIL IN HAIDA GWAII

West of British Columbia's west coast, beyond the boiling water of stormy dreams and on the knife's edge of the continental shelf, is a 280-kilometre-long archipelago of unsurpassed myth and beauty. A region of mountain, creeks, and towering trees, these Pacific islands are inhabited by a culture whose uniqueness means its art is instantly recognized, its language found nowhere else on Earth. When I set off to discover the best of Canada, I asked fellow travel writers what tops their own national bucket lists. More often than not, the answer was Haida Gwaii.

Flying into the sleepy village of Sandspit, I catch a ferry over to the $26-million Haida Cultural Centre to place my next adventure in some context. Here, I learn about the two Haida clans — Eagles and Ravens — and how they balance each other in marriage, trade, and even death. I learn about the importance of western red cedar, how imposing "totem" poles were carved to tell legends, honour men, and identify homesteads. I learn how this proud warrior nation, whose seafaring and ferocity have been compared to that of the Vikings, was all but exterminated after a century of European contact, in a deadly cocktail of disease and cultural genocide. Of the Haida who thrived on these islands, 95 percent disappeared, but their descendants are staging a remarkable comeback. First they reclaimed their art, which is recognized worldwide as a pinnacle of First Nations cultural expression. Next they reclaimed ownership of their land, in an unprecedented deal with the federal government, so that the Queen Charlotte Islands became Haida Gwaii (Place of the People). Now they are relearning their language, before it, too, becomes a ghost echoing in the forest.

It gives me a lot to think about as Moresby Explorer's 400-horse-power Zodiac speeds down the coast into the vast protected realms of Gwaii Haanas Marine Conservation Area Reserve and Haida Heritage Site. I am late for a date with Bluewater Adventures' twenty-one-metre-long *Island Roamer*, on which I will join a dozen tourists from around the country on a week-long sailing expedition. This 1,470-square-kilometre national park reserve, unique with its steward-ship from mountaintop to ocean floor, can only be accessed via boat and float plane. Only two thousand visitors are allowed each season. Founded in 1988, the reserve was a hard-fought victory for the Haida over political roadblocks and multinational logging companies busy shearing the islands of their forests.

I hop onboard to find new friends deeply fascinated with the cul-ture, wildlife, and beauty, and relishing the comfortable yacht in which to explore it. The islands of Gwaii Haanas boast forty endemic

The Day the Springs Sprung

On October 27, 2012, the largest earthquake to hit Canada in over six decades was recorded off the coast of Haida Gwaii. The massive offshore quake, which measured 7.7 on the Richter scale, rattled the region, but fortunately there was no damage to property or people. There was, however, a natural casualty. The hot springs in Gwaii Haanas National Park, located on the aptly named Hotspring Island, mysteriously dried up. Fault lines and fractures from the earthquake were blamed for the disappearance of this popular attraction. The good news: By June 2014, Parks Canada's heat-detecting devices showed hot water flowing above the tide line again. Locals and seismologists are optimistic the springs will return. ➤

species of animals and plants, is a haven for twenty-three types of whale and dozens of seabirds, and is covered with dense old-growth temperate rainforest. Sailing the calm waters between the coves and bays of the park's 138 islands, we spot humpbacks, seals, sea lions, and a large family of rare offshore orcas.

Bluewater's Zodiac or kayaks deposit us onshore to explore forests of giant western red cedar, hemlock, and Sitka spruce, the ground carpeted with bright green moss and fern. We walk among the ruins of an old whaling station in Rose Harbour and pick up Japanese garbage on Kunghit Island, blown in with the raging storms of the Pacific. In Echo Harbour, we watch schools of salmon launch themselves from the sea into the creek and a huge black bear (Haida Gwaii boasts the biggest black bears found anywhere) lick its lips in anticipation. We do the same on the yacht, with chef Deborah serving up fresh coconut-crusted halibut and other delights from her small but fully equipped galley.

As an eco-adventure, Gwaii Haanas deserves its reputation as a "Canadian Galapagos." Yet it's the legacy of the Haida themselves that elevates this wild, rugged coastline, a history best illustrated by the remarkable UNESCO World Heritage Site on Anthony Island, now known as SGang Gwaay. Haida lived here for millennia, but after the plague of smallpox, European trade, and residential schools, all that remains, fittingly, are eerie carved cedar mortuary poles. Facing the sea like sentinels with the thick forest at their backs, they make it an unforgettable and haunting place to visit, and all the more so for the effort it takes to do so. The five Haida village National Historic Sites in Gwaii Haannas — Skedans, Tanu, Windy Bay, Hotspring Island, and SGang Gwaay — are guarded by the Watchmen, local men and women employed by the community and Parks Canada.

James Williams has been a Watchman at SGang Gwaay for almost a decade, showing visitors around and enthusiastically describing the history of the village and the legacy of the poles. He tells us how the Haida attached supernatural qualities to the animals and trees that surrounded them, hence their culture borne out of tales featuring bears, ravens, eagles, killer whales, otters, and cedar. Unassuming in his baseball cap, James discusses violent battles with mainland tribes, the Haida acumen for trade, canoe building, and their interaction with European sea-otter traders, which ultimately killed off the animal and very nearly finished off the Haida themselves. Today, these weathered ash-grey mortuary poles are maintained to honour a tradition that once thrived and shows signs of thriving again. Tombstones that seem older than their 150-year-old origins, they remind me of the stone heads on Easter Island, the stone carvings of Angkor. Trees rattle in the onshore breeze as the forest slowly reclaims the remains of abandoned cedar longhouses. Isolated for months, James gifts us with some freshly caught halibut as he welcomes some arriving kayakers. With Watchmen having to live in solitude for months at a time, it is not so much a job as a calling.

Each abandoned village is different, and each Watchman reveals more about this rugged West Coast wonderland and the people who call it home. By the end of the week, both the land and its stewards have woven a spell over us. Designed to last the length of a single lifetime, old Haida totem poles will not last forever. Fortunately, the protection of Gwaii Haanas, by both the Haida people and Parks Canada, along with the deep respect paid to both by operators like Randy Burke's Bluewater Adventures, ensures this magical archipelago will remain on western Canada's Bucket List for generations to come.

START HERE: canadianbucketlist.com/haida

HIKE THE WEST COAST TRAIL

I'm overjoyed I experienced the West Coast Trail, but happier still that one of the world's great hikes didn't kill me. Hikers come from all over the world to challenge themselves on this rugged seventy-seven-kilometre trail. Shortly after I left the trailhead, I was convinced every one of them must be insane. Case in point: the few wild animals you might encounter are those most likely to eat you — bears, wolves, and cougars. The path is treacherous, the weather notorious, and every year about one hundred hikers are evacuated with injuries. Born out of a life-saving trail created alongside the Graveyard of the Pacific, where more than one thousand ships have run aground, the West Coast Trail is nonetheless a true Canadian challenge, in all its hurt and glory.

Tips for the Trail

Rub Vaseline on your feet every morning to avoid blisters

Pack more hot chocolate

Bring tea bags

Bring wraps to make meals go farther

Plastic bowls work better than plastic plates

A walking stick and gaiters are essential

Bring fire gloves for the campfire

Instant mash and rice works great as a meal

Don't bother with towels, a sarong will do

Bring knee or ankle guards if you think you might need them

Fruit bars are worth their weight in gold

A small bottle of hot sauce goes a long way

Bring an extra battery for your digital camera

If weather permits, take a day off and relax

Do your research

Speak to other hikers as you go for more info ➤

Snaking up the Pacific Rim National Park from Bamfield to Port Renfrew, you're far removed from roads, stores, or civilization. That's why park rangers patrol in helicopters and boats looking for wounded hikers suffering from sprains, slips, and hypothermia. Given that fifteen centimetres of rain can fall in just twelve hours, the well-marked trail can quickly become a quagmire of thick mud, sharp rocks, and slippery boardwalks. So why would anyone actually add this to their bucket list? To find out, I joined a group of seven hikers, allocating our supplies according to our body weights. All our trash would have to be burned or carried out, while lunch would consist only of GORP (granola-oatmeal-raisin-peanut) and energy bars.

Within the first exhausting hour, evacuation didn't seem like such a bad idea. The rain was holding off, but the path was streaked with roots and knee-deep mud pools. Then came the wooden ladders, some of which climb as high as twenty-five metres.

Top 10 Hikes in Western Canada

In 2014, Parks Canada opened up a third official access point on the West Coast Trail at Nitinat Narrows. Located nearly halfway along the trail, the narrows is one of the few spots where you can buy a snack and have a local boat you fifty metres across some nasty rapids to the other side. It's also a popular spot for evacuations. The new access point makes exits easier, and also allows up to eight hikers a day to hop on the trail for a shorter trip.

In a region blessed with incredible hikes and trails, here are some of the best:

1. West Coast Trail, BC
2. Skyline Trail, AB
3. Heiko's Trail, BC
4. Crypt Lake, AB
5. Juan de Fuca Trail, BC
6. Tonquin Valley Trail, AB
7. Stawamus Chief, BC
8. Larch Valley-Sentinel Pass, AB
9. Chilkoot Trail, BC
10. Northover Ridge, AB

With my knees creaking under the weight of my twenty-five-kilogram backpack, I stumble into camp seven hours later, collapsing in a heap.

"The nice thing about hurting your ankle is you forget how much your back and feet hurt," says my friend Andrew, who is dealing with a sprained ankle and receiving absolutely no sympathy. Each man's pain is his own. The key to success, according to Kyle, our veteran hiker, is preparation. We have all the essentials: walking sticks, gaiters, camel packs, dehydrated food, good tents, a water pump.

"Inexperienced hikers are usually the first to go," a park ranger tells me. "This is not the trail to break in new boots."

We build our campfires beside driftwood benches and bathe in freezing streams. All food is locked in communal bear lockers overnight, and one morning we awake to find fresh wolf prints next to the tent, just in case we thought we were alone. Halfway into the week-long hike, my pack begins to lighten and my muscles harden. I stop kvetching long enough to admire the massive Douglas fir trees, the sea arches, limestone cliffs, waterfalls, sandy beaches, crystal tidal pools bristling with luminous purple starfish and green anemones. The camaraderie with fellow hikers from around the world, met along the way or in camp, tops up this natural inspiration. Sharing tips on what to expect up ahead, we're all pushing our mental and physical limits. Each day we hike between eleven and seventeen kilometres of challenging terrain.

At the end of the week, food consumed and camera batteries low, I trudge along the final twelve kilometres to the end, grateful for the extra-strength painkillers. Our group is haggard, dirty, sore — and utterly elated. "Few finish this adventure pain-free," reads a popular hiking website.

Why is the West Coast Trail on the bucket list? For the challenge, the beauty, the communal spirit, and the opportunity to say, "Yes, I did it, and it didn't kill me!"

START HERE: canadianbucketlist.com/wct

DIVE A SUNKEN BATTLESHIP

With the press of a button, I descend into the cold, dark murk of the Pacific. It's a far cry from the warm turquoise waters of Papua New Guinea, where I learned to scuba dive among hundreds of tropical fish. Yet the waters off the coast of Vancouver Island are renowned for offering some of the best diving on the planet, with no less an authority than the late Jacques Cousteau rating B.C. as the second-best temperate dive spot in the world, behind the Red Sea.

To see if he was right, if emerald oceans can compete with sapphire seas, I will have to adapt. In these cold waters, dry suits are a necessity, as they allow you to remain dry in an airtight bubble, adjusting descent and ascent through air valves. This kind of diving also requires extra training, which is why I call on Greg McCracken, one of B.C.'s top instructors, to introduce me to the submersible wonders of Canada.

What makes the diving so special in B.C. is how big everything is. Orange sunflower starfish the size of dinner tables, forests of bright white plumose anemones, giant octopus, wolf eels, and big-eyed cabezons. Forget the tropics; divers in B.C. immerse themselves in the clear, clean waters of another planet — and you can keep your jeans on. Greg picked out one of the most spectacular dives on offer: the sunken destroyer HMCS *Saskatchewan*, sitting upright on the ocean floor not far from the ferry port of Vancouver Island's Departure Bay. The Artificial Reef Society of B.C. is a world leader in the art of creating environmentally protective reefs, having sunk six ships and one Boeing 737 in B.C. waters. Such reefs attract indigenous marine life, creating a sustainable and attractive destination for scuba divers.

It's a crisp early morning when Sea Dragon Charters' dive boat anchors to a buoy alongside a slither of rock and sand called Snake Island, home to 250 harbour seals. Two huge bald eagles soar above us. We suit up, bulked by our layers, resembling alien superheroes attached to all manner of pipes and tanks. Even though the water is a brisk seven degrees Celsius, I'm surprised at how insulated and comfortable dry suits can be. After descending twenty metres, we see the first anemones, rocking in the breeze of the ocean currents. A huge lingcod is perfectly camouflaged against the reef. I soon realize the reef is, in fact, metal, part of the 111-metre-long *Mackenzie*-class destroyer. Our flippers propel us forward, and I see the old canons, now exploding with marine life. There are huge spiky copper rockfish, purple California sea cucumbers, assorted sculpins, and thousands of dancing brittlestars. Two hundred and thirty officers

British Columbia's Top Dives

Greg and Deirdre McCracken, owners of B.C.'s Ocean Quest Diving Centre and two of the province's most respected divers, list their Top 10.

1. Browning Wall (boat dive) — Port Hardy
2. Skookumchuck Rapids (boat dive) — Egmont
3. Steep Island (boat dive) — Campbell River
4. Rentate Reef (boat dive) — Barkley Sound
5. Dodd Narrows (boat dive) — Nanaimo
6. Race Rocks (boat dive) — Victoria
7. HMCS *Saskatchewan* (boat dive) — Nanaimo
8. Wreck of the *Capilano* (boat dive) — Comox
9. Whytecliff Park (shore dive) — Vancouver
10. Ogden Point (shore dive) — Victoria

once lived aboard this ship. Since it was sunk in 1997, local marine life has gladly taken the officers' place.

We swim through the control deck, descending to twenty-nine metres before making our way back to the midship buoy, keeping an eye on our air supply. After making the required safety stops to avoid decompression sickness, we climb on board the boat elated. "The size and abundance of marine life in B.C. really sets it apart," explains Greg over hot chocolate. "You experience things underwater here that you just can't experience anywhere else."

Just a few hundred feet away from the battleship is another artificial wreck, the world's second-largest upright reef and one of B.C.'s most popular diving locations. The HMCS *Cape Breton* is a 134-metre-long Second World War Victory ship, built for action in 1944 but converted into an escort and maintenance ship soon after. After languishing for decades, she was cleaned up and sunk upright onto a flat seabed off Snake Island in 2001. Once again we suit up, check our air pressure, add weights to our belts. The *Cape Breton* is a massive wreck to explore and cannot be done in one dive. You feel like a budgie exploring a double-decker bus. Greg hand signals to a long corridor, and I follow him through it, peering with my flashlight into various rooms, noticing the fish, plants, and sponges that have moved in. We hover over the engine room skylights, but as much as I'd like to explore the playground below, Greg warned me that this area is only for technical, well-trained divers. When you're thirty metres below the surface connected to life by an oxygen tank, it's best not to argue.

A half-hour later, we ascend once more to the warm tea and smiles of the *Sea Dragon* crew. They're used to huge smiles lighting up the faces of divers emerging from the depths of British Columbia.

Note: Diving should only be attempted with the proper training, available across the country. If you have chronic ear problems, as I do, look into a product called Docs Pro-Plugs. These handy vented plugs are worth their weight in underwater treasure.

START HERE: canadianbucketlist.com/scuba

SURF IN TOFINO

Canada may be a cold northern country, but Canadians can still live for the surf, philosophize about the rhythm of the ocean, and call each other "dude." Tofino is not Malibu or Haleiwa, but then Vancouver Island is not California or Hawaii. This laid-back surf town demands a commitment to the waves, not sun-bleached hair and bikinis. When you surf in a full-body wetsuit, pretentiousness dissipates.

The town sits on the wild west coast of Vancouver Island, battered by volatile weather that washes up debris along its long sandy beaches, shredding trees in the surrounding Pacific Rim National Park. Storm

Surf's Up

After renting your gear and taking a lesson with one of Tofino's six surf schools, head to one of these popular surf spots:

Cox Bay: One and a half kilometres long, facing west, the most consistent break in the area and probably the most popular surf destination in the country.

Florencia Bay: Five kilometres long, facing mostly south, one of the quieter beaches, with a steep shoreline offering protection from cold westerly winds.

Chesterman Beach: Popular beach with locals and families, with forgiving swells that make it one of the best beginner breaks on the continent.

Wickaninnish Beach: Located at the south end of the sixteen-kilometre, aptly named Long Beach, it faces west and has an epic coastline. ➤

watching is a popular pastime in the spring and fall, best enjoyed from the large picture windows of the Wickaninnish Inn, one of the finest hotels in the country. Tofino offers whale watching, hot springs, artisans, and hikes in old-growth forest, and for Canadians embracing surf culture, there's no better place to be. Although the climate can be extreme, the surf community is unusually friendly. The beach break is kind to beginners, and one of the most popular local surf schools is called Surf Sisters. Visitors from southern surf towns enjoy the fact that territorial testosterone is kept to a minimum.

Insulated from head to toe, I enter the ten-degree-Celsius water. Although waves can reach up to ten metres, today is a gentle introduction to the art of riding them. Just several metres into the waters of Cox Bay, I sit on board and admire the unkempt beach cradled by a wind-battered forest. There are no bars, clothing stores, or hard

bodies glistening in the sun. Instead of birds in bikinis, a bald eagle soars overhead. It's my first time on a surfboard, and while the waves may be timid, I still spend the afternoon wiping out, falling off my long board with the grace of a flying ostrich. When I do stand up, for just a moment, the heavens sing hallelujah, and an eagle swoops by to give me a congratulatory wink. Maybe I've swallowed too much of the Pacific and I'm not thinking straight. What does it matter? Without the attitude and pushiness, sans the ego and tan lines, surfing the wilderness of Vancouver Island keeps your soul warm just as surely as a wetsuit. Even if you don't manage to get up.

START HERE: canadianbucketlist.com/tofino

TRACK THE SPIRIT BEAR

Pacific Northwest Airlines' amphibious Grumman Goose splashes down, and clearly the Great Bear Rainforest is in good spirits. Absent on this fine mid-September afternoon is the notorious west coast weather, replaced by a beaming sun striking the Pacific Ocean like a spotlight on a mirror ball. What's more, the familiar face I'd seen

ON THE BUCKET LIST: Wade Davis

Todagin Mountain, a wildlife sanctuary in the sky that anchors the nine headwater lakes of the Iskut River, main tributary of the Stikine. Todagin is home to the largest concentration of Stone sheep in the world. Because the herd is resident in all seasons, the mountain is also home to an astonishing number of predators: grizzly and wolf, black bear and wolverine. So rich are the wildlife values that hunting by rifle has been forbidden for decades. Unfortunately, open-pit copper and gold mining on the very flank of the mountain threatens to bury pristine lakes in toxic tailings. See Todagin while you still can, and if enough Canadians do, perhaps we might still stop this egregious violation of the Tahltan homeland.

Wade Davis
Author, Explorer in Residence
National Geographic Society

at the Vancouver airport's south terminal is coming along for the ride, a man who passionately knows this area, and its conservation, better than most: David Suzuki, Canada's most respected environmentalist.

Guests are arriving from around the world to explore this unspoiled temperate rainforest, stretching seventy thousand square kilometres from northern British Columbia to the Alaska border. Within its boundaries are hundreds of islands, dozens of First Nations communities, vast amounts of wildlife, and one peculiar animal that has long captured the public imagination — a bear with a coat as white as snow that roams the forest creeks like a mist in search of substance. A bear so rare that fewer than one thousand are said to exist, and with a spirit so powerful it has never been hunted or trapped. This rare kermode bear, commonly known as the spirit bear, has a recessive gene that gives this subspecies its distinctive white coat. Not an albino, not a different species, just a family of black rainforest bears that pass on a trait that gives them a distinct appearance, like a tribe of redheads living in the Amazon.

We settle into our fishing lodge, pampered by staff, enjoying outstanding cuisine, gorgeous views, and cozy wooden surroundings. Some of us have arrived with the hopes of hooking giant halibut, or

hiking into the mountains among the old growth trees. Others are here to see the hundreds of humpback, orca, and fin whales that feed in the rich sea channels. We can also visit the Git Ga'at, the closest First Nations community, to meet elders and learn about their fascinating culture in Hartley Bay. Or pop over to a unique, isolated whale research station to hear eerie hydrophonic songs of local migratory whales. But a different mammal is the star attraction at this time of year. Each September, when millions of salmon begin their final journey up the very creeks in which they were born, the great bears that give the region its name come out to feast.

It's an hour-long boat ride along the tidal zone of Princess Royal, crossing the whitecaps on the channel that separates it from our destination: Gribbell Island. Docking against the rocks, we are greeted by a man who has lived and worked with the spirit bears his entire life. Marven Robinson is the go-to guy for the kermode, the man who introduces film crews, tourists, and journalists to this magical animal. Marven personally constructed wooden platforms along Riordan Creek in places that least disturb the bears but still allow visitors to observe them in their natural habitat. "I'm here to protect the bears," he says, "not the people."

Supplied with sandwiches and hot soup, we begin the wait. Marven talks about his passion for protecting he bears, and how hunting black bears with recessive genes is a major threat to the kermode. David Suzuki tells me about the fight to save the region from becoming an oil supertanker highway, and how, despite huge financial incentives, the First Nations have joined conservationists to say enough is enough: protecting Great Bear's natural resources is more important than a short-term paycheque. All this happens in jarringly beautiful surroundings, reminding me of those idyllic photo wallpapers so popular back in the 1970s, the kind that depicted the tranquil forest of your dreams.

Below us, hundreds of pink salmon are spawning, squirming against one another, darting upstream. It's the abundance of this food source that Marven knows will draw the bears, eventually. In the meantime, we talk *sotto voce*, swatting the bugs away from our faces.

Finally, I feel a ripple of excitement. A large black bear is making its way downstream. It stops, swipes a mouthful of salmon from a pool, and tears it to pieces. Slowly, the bear ambles along the river, stopping right beneath our platform, oblivious to our quiet presence. Privileged to be a guest at a spectacle that takes place all over the coast, I hear the sound of memory cards filling up, and then an excited whisper: "There it is!"

A large kermode male, all 135 kilos of him, six years old by Marven's reckoning, is following in the footsteps of the black bear. Ethereal, pink-nosed, with cream-white fur at odds with the earthy tones of its surroundings, the kermode chases salmon in the pools, spraying drops of water that reflect the early afternoon sunlight. Suddenly the black bear charges aggressively, sending the kermode into the mossy bank adjacent to our platform. Unperturbed, it re-enters a few metres downstream and continues its hunt for, as I'm told, as many as eighty fish a day. Finally, both bears wander off, leaving us spellbound by our good fortune. There's no guarantee you'll see the spirit bear on any given day, and more than once on my Canadian journey I've found myself facing the wrong end of the barrel of fortune. But not today.

Welcome to New Caledonia

I once visited a friend on a little slice of France located 16,000 kilometres east of Europe, in the South Pacific. Governed in Paris, New Caledonia has tropical beaches, strong cheese, great wine and locals who can't quite believe their luck at having been born in such a place. It could have been ours . . . the name anyway. Simon Fraser originally wanted to call the new British crown colony on the Pacific coast "New Caledonia," since the mountains reminded him of the Scottish Highlands. Alas, Queen Victoria nipped that idea in the bud, as Captain James Cook had already claimed his New Caledonia in the South Pacific. ➤

The First Nations have always protected the spirit bear, believing it has a powerful effect on all who are lucky enough to see it. My encounter left me inspired by the power of true wilderness, along with all the creatures that inhabit it, protect it, and nurture its future. Creatures like the Git Ga'at, Marven Robinson, and David Suzuki. Creatures like our local guide George's granny (with her "sixty-five-plus grandkids!") and the couple who live in isolation at a whale research station. Creatures like the kermode, which radiates magic, bring it all together.

START HERE: canadianbucketlist.com/spiritbear

SNORKEL WITH SALMON

Next time you order sushi, spare a thought for the miracle of Canada's Pacific salmon. Half a billion of them, returning from a five-thousand-kilometre journey in the open ocean, ready to spawn in the very gravel, in the very river, where they themselves once hatched. In the process, they must survive a who's who of salmon addicts — seals, sharks, eagles, sea lions, bears — and, of course, human appetites. Leaping from pond to pond, battling predators, starvation, suffocation, overcrowding, and fierce interspecies competition, their backs hump, their noses hook, and their skin turns red as finally they are ready to mate. Having accomplished this extraordinary feat of derring-do, they promptly die. Why these kamikaze pilots are drawn to the rivers of British Columbia is still something of a mystery (Atlantic salmon don't die after mating), but it certainly has

something to do with B.C.'s abundance of fresh water, filtered by its wealth of temperate rainforest. As the spent bodies of salmon wash downstream, they continue to feed up to two hundred species in the forest. Some 80 percent of the nitrogen found in forest soil can be traced to salmon, nitrogen vital for hemlock, spruce, and cedar to grow. Delicious as they may be (smoked, barbecued, fried, or grilled), there simply wouldn't be a B.C. without its annual salmon run. A salmon run you can witness first-hand, underwater, each year with Destiny River Adventures in Campbell River.

Suiting up in full-body wetsuits for a two-hour journey downstream, Jamie Turko and his crew transport us on whitewater rafts to the base of the river. A hydroelectric project regulates the Campbell River's water supply, making it a particularly safe river in which to do what we're about to do. Which is: hop in the water with masks and snorkels, point our arms downriver, float with the current, and immerse ourselves in this little-seen world of salmon — hundreds of thousands of them.

Jamie, who has run salmon snorkelling tours for over two decades, explains the differences between the five species: the mighty chinook, the chum, the sockeye, coho, and pink. We'll mostly be seeing pink salmon today, interspersed with giant chinooks, along with opportunist rainbow and steelhead trout (yet another predator for nature's ultimate survivors). This enormous bounty of fish means we won't be alone. Locals line the banks with their rods, catching their seasonal quota, or catch-and-releasing in hopes of hooking a true beast (a 32-kilogram chinook was caught in the area in 2010). Locals watch us with a mix of curiosity and envy, for once we enter the brisk

Acquiring a Taste for Salmon

Packed with protein, omega-3 fatty acids, vitamins and minerals, a diet rich in salmon is considered to be an extremely healthy one. Salmon is cited as being beneficial for everything from arthritis and dry skin to heart disease and Alzheimer's. But when it comes to cooking, the five species of Pacific salmon are not created equal. Ask any local and they'll tell you: the firm, pink, and oily sockeye swims way ahead of the pack. ➤

current of the river, we can see exactly where the fish are. And boy, they are everywhere.

Wetsuits suitably disarm the 10°C water as we enter the river. From above, I had seen streaks of grey darting in the green-brown water. Underwater, there are salmon everywhere — walls of them, floors of them, cities and towns and planets of them. Despite the obstacles that began the moment they were born, in just one corner I see enough survivors to assuage a feeling of guilt. Certain stocks are threatened, and the debate over farmed salmon versus wild rages on, but today there seems to be a fish for every Tom, Dick, and hungry Harry.

We raft over some gentle rapids and enter another section of the river, where the current carries us into more schools with a feeling that is part buoyancy, part flying. For a moment I feel like a fish myself, nervously watching for rocks, large predators, and deceptive bait. Most of all, though, I'm just having fun, in awe of a fish that deserves credit for shaping the environment of the West Coast; a fish that, against all the odds, finds itself on the Great Western Canada Bucket List.

START HERE: canadianbucketlist.com/salmon

LISTEN TO BOB MARLEY IN A COLD SAUNA

You, too, can enjoy the health benefits of freezing to death. And benefits there must be, otherwise guests wouldn't pay for what they're paying for at Sparkling Hill, a pretty, Austrian-style resort located near the interior town of Vernon. Owned by the Swarovski family and adorned with $10 million worth of their crystals, Sparkling Hill has an ambience that is distinctly Old World Luxury, even with the crystal fireplaces, stunning pools, and themed steam rooms in the award-winning KurSpa. I'm wooing my wife with these facts in the four seconds it takes before her panic attack sets in. To be fair, we are half naked in a small room with the temperature a frosty -60°C. Sorry, that's the second room; her real panic attack hit in the third room, at -110°C. Hey, she's Brazilian, they freeze to death quicker than the rest of us.

How We Freeze to Death

As soon as your body gets cold, blood moves away from your skin and extremities to protect your core. Shivering is a mechanism to generate warmth, and it gets intense once your core temperature begins to sink. Welcome to hypothermia. The good news is that hypothermia is typically associated with moisture (our bodies lose heat about twenty-five times faster in water than in air), which is why the cold sauna is so well insulated, air current free, and perfectly dry.

When the body temperature drops from its normal 37°C, horrible things start to happen. Lose five degrees and you'll lose consciousness. Once you hit 21°C, your lights might go out permanently. Inside Sparkling Hill's cold sauna, sticking around longer than the prescribed and therapist-monitored three minutes is a bad idea. Just two to three minutes in, your body surface temperature plummets to -2°C, but your core remains comfortable. Once your time is up, relief, warmth, and comfort are just steps away. ➤

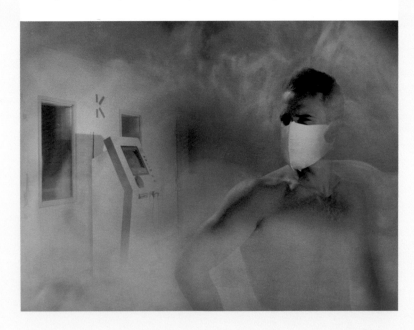

A visit to North America's first cold sauna provides a treatment in something called cryotherapy, which activates biochemical, hormonal, and immune processes to give your circulatory and nervous systems a healthy kick-start. Sports stars apparently swear by it, whereas I was just swearing, deeply, under my breath, while my eyelashes froze and my nasal passage turned to ice. Strictly monitored, my wife and I are told to wear bathing suits, supplemented with gloves and slippers. In order to prevent any humidity, we enter the cold sauna through three separate rooms: the first a balmy -15°C, the second -60°C, and the final corker -110°C. Here we must walk in small circles for three minutes, encouraged by a bundled-up spa worker. Ever jump into a freezing cold lake? Multiply the shock by ten, and go ahead and punch yourself in the neck for good measure. My wife freaks out, and the spa worker quickly ushers her out to safety.

Meanwhile, I continue walking with three elderly ladies in a tight circle, all of us trying not to touch each other in case we fuse.

Bob Marley is blasting from in-sauna speakers, "stirring it up," as it were, with images of frozen corpses washing up on the beach. As I twitch with cold, nipples ready to break off, my testicles having retreated deep into my pancreas, the three minutes come to an end and we rush out of the chamber. Time may fly when you're having fun, but when you're freezing to death, a single Bob Marley song can sound like a James Joyce reading. Here's the best part: once you exit the cold sauna, you are not allowed to hop in a hot tub or steam room. I assume it's because the rush of blood would explode your head like a champagne cork. Rather, we are told to rest in our robes and drink a warm cup of tea.

While you need multiple treatments (sold in blocks of ten) for the cryotherapy to be effective — flash-freezing muscle inflammation, improving joint and muscle function, and relieving skin irritation—one visit was perfectly adequate for my purposes. My wife did (eventually) forgive me, and once again I learned that what doesn't kill you only makes you appreciate the bizarre things people pay good money for.

START HERE: canadianbucketlist.com/coldsauna

EXPLORE AN OLD-GROWTH FOREST

These days, it's hard to impress kids who have grown up on PlayStation, music videos, and television cocktails spiked with attention deficit disorder. Show them a great mountain, a sweeping beach, a lush forest, and chances are they'll be glued to their text messages on the cellphone you regretted the minute you bought it for them. Fortunately, Mother Nature still has some tricks up her foliage when it comes to impressing children, and it's doubtful cellphone coverage will interfere at all. Yes, they're just trees, kids. But look at the size of them!

The giant red cedars, Douglas firs, hemlocks, and spruce trees that survive in the old-growth forests of British Columbia are truly

BRITISH COLUMBIA ↑

Canada's Biggest Trees

According to the Ancient Forest Alliance, the town of Port Renfrew is the go-to place if you're looking for the biggest trees in Canada. Near this Vancouver Island town you can find the planet's biggest Douglas fir and biggest spruce tree, as well as the biggest tree in the country, the Cheewhat cedar. Located within the Pacific Rim National Park Reserve, the Cheewhat is 56 metres high, 6 metres in trunk diameter, and has enough timber volume to create 450 regular telephone poles' worth of wood. ➤

impressive. Somehow, these trees have survived the colonial building boom and the modern logging industry, and now range in age between 250 and over 1,000 years old. "This tree was here before Marco Polo explored China, before Shakespeare . . . em, before Harry Potter!" Fantasy is an apt means to capture a kid's imagination, because standing between 800-year-old Douglas fir trees — towering up to seventy-five metres high in Cathedral Grove in Vancouver Island's MacMillan Provincial Park — you can't help but feel you're on another planet. The forest moon of Endor comes to mind, although I'm dating myself with *Star Wars*. Perhaps the kids will prefer Avatar Grove, fifteen minutes away from Port Renfrew, so named for this ancient red cedar and Douglas fir forest's resemblance to the planet Pandora in the blockbuster *Avatar*. Surrounded by a drapery of ferns and moss, with a soundtrack of chattering woodpeckers or bubbling brooks, a spell of peace and space envelops adults as well. When the kids get tired of trying to hug a trunk that can accommodate the linked hands of eight people, bedazzle them with a contorted red cedar known as "Canada's Gnarliest Tree." Keeping with the theme, it looks remarkably like Jabba the Hut.

According to the Ancient Forest Alliance, a B.C. organization working to protect these natural wonders (and support sustainable forestry practices), less than 25 percent of the old-growth forest on Vancouver Island still exists, and only 10 percent of the biggest trees that you might find on a valley bottom. Some studies have shown that conserving old-growth trees might be more economically viable than slicing them

down for furniture. Meanwhile, the few remaining stands in the province are still threatened with clear-cutting, including Avatar Grove. The emotional and childlike wonder that accompanies hiking an old-growth forest certainly belongs on our Bucket List. Unfortunately, we have to add the caveat: "while they still exist."

START HERE: canadianbucketlist.com/oldgrowth

BIKE WHERE THE PIGS ARE FLYING

British Columbia offers some of the world's best downhill mountain biking. Whistler, Fernie, Rossland, Vancouver's North Shore ... so why is the small town of Burns Lake on my bucket list? Well, local bikers were once told that Burns Lake would have a world-class bike park when pigs fly. Well, the today the pigs are soaring at Burns Lake Trails, a biker's paradise built by the same folks behind the Whistler Mountain Bike Park.

The upper slopes of Boer Mountain are clawed with twisting single-track dirt trails, challenging wooden ramps, berms, loops, and switchbacks. Bikers are served by a shuttle service that runs to the top, and you'll quickly discover that the trails also benefit from the welcoming community spirit of Burns Lake. Racing down tracks with names like Piglet, Smells like Bacon, and When Pigs Fly, I'm reminded of an old saying: Those who say it can't be done should get out of the way of those who are doing it.

START HERE: canadianbucketlist.com/downhillbike

GO HELI-SKIING

Welcome to a place where a person's worth is measured in vertical feet. It is surrounded by mountains, waist-high powder, and the *whomp-whomp* sound of a helicopter. Heli-skiing has been on my bucket list ever since I discovered how much fun it is to strap on a plank of polyethylene and launch oneself off a mountain. Having gone through the meat grinder of learning to snowboard, the idea of being dropped off at the top of the world to float over virgin snow seems a just reward. Thus I found myself at the Canadian Mountain Holiday's K2 Rotor Lodge in Nakusp, among a group of Americans on a Mancation, folks proudly addicted to the "other" white powder. How else to explain the guy celebrating his six-millionth vertical foot with CMH? Or the sole Canadian who has visited every one of CMH's eleven heli-skiing lodges? Using a helicopter as a makeshift ski chair doesn't come cheap, with trips costing north of six thousand

Tips for Heli-Skiing

- The more fit you are, the more fun you will have. Start training as early as possible, focusing on cardio and muscle strength.
- Make sure your boots are worn in and comfy. This is not the place to break in a new pair. And make sure you pack them in your carry-on luggage, just in case.
- CMH veterans sing the praises of yoga classes as having increased core strength and flexibility, improving their skiing.
- Drink water on every heli-run. Keep those muscles hydrated and prevent fatigue.
- The free stretch classes before breakfast are gold. Warm up and iron out the stiffness before each day begins.
- Book off enough time to get used to the powder and physical demands, so you can truly enjoy the magic heli-skiing delivers. ➤

dollars. "My wife goes on cruises, I go to the mountains," explains Mike. One guy has flown in from London, England, for four days of powder. That's if the weather plays ball.

It's late February, and the avalanche risk is high. The snow is plentiful, but conditions mean "we only have an area about eight times the size of Whistler available to us, as opposed to one hundred times," explains affable mountain guide Rob.

We watch a safety video, which pretty much explains all the ways heli-skiing can kill you: avalanches, tree wells, decapitation by skis. We practise avalanche drills and rescue, get fitted with receivers, radios, and shovels, and finally head to the Bell chopper we will come to know so well. I see grown adults behave like little kids, clapping their hands with glee. Wind, visibility, and terrain dictate where the helicopter can land, but it appears to be able to settle gently on pretty well anything. We exit, the chopper taking off right over our heads, and the Selkirk Mountains surround us in blue-sky mountain glory.

I strap in, barely containing my excitement, and proceed to have the worst run of my life. Powder, I discover, is not a groomed ski hill. Heli-skiing and -riding require new techniques, new muscles and instincts. My group of heli-veterans patiently pull me out of tree wells, traverses, and snow burials. Every muscle is burning as I battle my physical demons, determined to master the challenge. This is why you don't go heli-skiing for one day. Besides bad weather that can ground you for days, you need several days to enjoy the diversity of runs and snow, and to progress in your ability. We ski runs called Drambuie and Cognac, In Too Deep, Lobster Claw, and, my favourite, Little Leary. I had expected just a few rides in the helicopter, but we average about ten a day, the pilot somehow landing the copter just a few feet from our heads for the return flight to the top of the mountain. Like the skiing itself, it's a thrill that doesn't get tired. We whoop and bird-call through the forest, making sure nobody is lost, over fresh powder that stretches in every direction.

By day three, I've found my groove. Early morning stretching classes (and fabulous food) at the lodge help the muscle woes, and now I'm carving in deep pow, slaloming pine and hemlock trees. "That was the best run so far," says the guy from England after just about every run. I'm taken with the routine of each day: wake up, stretch, eat, ski, soak in natural hot springs, drink beer, eat dinner, retire early. No wonder these guys keep coming back, and work so hard to be able to afford to do so.

Atop a mountain on the final day, crystals glittering in the air as skis click into their bindings, I soak in a post-adrenalin, post-exhaustion, sense-of-achievement high. It's been a once-in-a-lifetime week of sport, companionship and natural beauty. A highlight on the Great Western Bucket List, and my first fifty thousand feet of CMH vertical. Strap in, there's still a long way to go.

START HERE: canadianbucketlist.com/heliski

STOP AND SMELL THE ROSES

Receiving around one million visitors each year, Vancouver Island's iconic Butchart Gardens is a National Historic Site and a stunning depiction of flora as art. Set on fifty-five acres of privately owned land near Victoria, the gardens date back to 1904.

Having exhausted a limestone quarry for the family's successful business, matriarch Jennie Butchart was determined to restore the natural beauty of the area. Anyone who steps into her ivy-coated Sunken Garden can see just how seriously she took the task. Today, more than fifty gardeners maintain the immaculate Butchart Gardens, well-deserving of their world-renowned reputation. Open year round, flowers and bulbs change with the seasons, blossoming by the thousands in spring, glowing in summer, radiating red and gold in the

Top 10 Places to See Flowers in Western Canada

Have a fancy for the floral? Water your passion with these options in
western Canada:

1. Butchart Gardens, Victoria, BC
2. Vancouver Cherry Blossom Festival, BC
3. Tulips of the Valley, Seabird Island, BC
4. Waterton Wild Flower Festival, AB
5. Manning Provincial Park wildflowers, BC
6. Bradner Daffodil Festival, Bradner, BC
7. Queen Elizabeth Park, Vancouver, BC
8. Prairie Gardens, Edmonton, AB
9. Nikka Yuko Japanese Garden, Lethbridge, AB
10. Dr. Sun Yat-Sen Classical Chinese Garden, Vancouver, BC

fall. On-site restaurants and tea gardens keep visitors satiated; while a delightful carousel brings out the kid in everyone (I think I enjoyed it more than my fourteen-month-old). Most visitors spend about ninety minutes exploring the various gardens, but if you're not in a rush, take a blanket with you and stop to relax in the sunshine, surrounded by dancing bees and a riot of colour. Don't miss the Japanese Garden, the Italian Garden, the Rose Garden, live music performances, and popular Saturday evening fireworks.

START HERE: canadianbucketlist.com/butchartgardens

BRITISH COLUMBIA ↑

POWDER DOWN IN WHISTLER

When it comes to North America's largest and most highly rated ski resort, one word comes to mind: *epic*. Epic terrain. Epic snow. Epic dining. Between Whistler and the adjacent mountain, Blackcomb, you've got 8,100 acres of skiable terrain linked by the world's longest and highest lift system, the 4.4-kilometre-long Peak2Peak. That's over 50 percent more terrain than any other ski resort on the continent, and the reason you'll find long lineups with visitors from around the world. To ensure the first line of the day will be mine, I pick up a Fresh Tracks ticket, which offers a breakfast buffet and early loading privileges at the top of the mountain. I've still got egg in my mouth when I hear "The runs are open!" This initiates

Western Canada's Top 10 Ski Resorts

Scott Birke, editor of Snowboard Magazine Canada, *drops in the ultimate Canadian ski and snowboard destinations.*

1. **Whistler Blackcomb, BC:** For its two massive mountains with more than two hundred runs, world-class terrain parks, and some of the best slackcountry in the world.
2. **Red Mountain, BC:** Since you can drop in anywhere 360° from the top, and as long as you don't go below the mid-mountain cat track, you're good to go.
3. **Whitewater, BC:** The trees over on Glory Ridge are so perfectly spaced and free of people that you'd think you're out of bounds.
4. **Fernie, BC:** Big bowls, tons of gullies to slash and lots of snow? No-brainer here.
5. **Lake Louise, AB:** For some of the most majestic views ever and its great expansive terrain.
6. **Sun Peaks, BC:** With five hundred acres of new terrain, Canada's second-largest ski resort boasts three mountains, long runs, hikeable slackcountry, incredible glades, dry snow, and accessible amenities.
7. **Kicking Horse, BC:** Sixty percent of its runs are rated black and double-black. 'Nuff said.
8. **Revelstoke Mountain Resort, BC:** At 5,620 feet of vertical, it's the highest drop in Canada. Oh, and it gets tons of snow.
9. **Sunshine Village, Banff, AB/BC:** Wanna test your mettle? Sunshine has two words for you: Delirium Dive, which requires full avalanche gear to access.
10. **Big White, Kelowna, BC:** Family-friendly with a side of champagne pow, Big White is the epitome of ski-in, ski-out, with almost all accommodations on-hill. ➤

a school bell–like atmosphere as everyone grabs their gear and races off to Emerald Express.

Having only discovered snowboarding in my late twenties, I still get a kick taking lift rides surrounded by shark-fin alpine peaks. Among the kids are adults with permission to behave like children, whooping at the top of the world and then bulleting down the mountain on planks of fibreglass. I'm not one for throwing myself into the challenging Double Diamond bowls, although there's plenty of that to go around. Rather, I choose to glide down the blues, in seventh heaven on my favourite runs: Harmony Ridge, Peak to Creek, the Saddle, and Spanky's. Riding the impressive Peak2Peak Gondola can be unnerving, especially in the glass-bottom carriage. The reward is worth it. Blackcomb offers heaps of snow, with accurately named runs like Jersey Cream and, yes, Seventh Heaven.

The entire experience has a tendency to make other resorts pale in comparison. No wonder so many visitors return year after year, or simply pack up and move here for good. Factor in the nightlife, festivals, world-class restaurants — Barefoot Bistro's nitro ice cream is something to experience on its own, as is their $1.4-million wine cellar — along with endless backcountry Nordic trails and thrills at the Whistler Bobsleigh Centre, and it's always a powder day for Whistler on the Western Canada Bucket List.

START HERE: canadianbucketlist.com/whistler

FLY LIKE A SUPERHERO BETWEEN THE PEAKS

Ziplining typically takes place through forest or canopy, and is safe enough for your grandmother, if she hasn't tried it already. Superfly, located just an eight-minute drive from Whistler Village, elevates the thrills. These ziplines, Canada's longest, let you fly backcountry-style between the soaring peaks of Cougar and Rainbow Mountain. Even better, all the lines are tandem, so you can share the experience with a partner, friend, parent, or child.

Using a comfortable harness more familiar to hang gliders, hold on to a bar or go hands-free as you clock in at speeds of more than one hundred kilometres per hour. As you break free of the forest canopy, the scenery is simply astounding and the flight is unforgettable. *Is it a bird? A plane?* No, it's just you.

START HERE: canadianbucketlist.com/superfly

SOAK IN THE LIARD HOT SPRINGS

Thermal activity beneath British Columbia has gifted the province with a selection of outstanding hot springs. Located a twenty-five-minute drive south of Radium, Fairmont is the country's largest, renowned for its healing waters devoid of the sulphur stink. The resort also features golf courses, shopping, dining, and a ski area. Size may or may not matter (depending on who you speak to), but I prefer Canada's second-largest springs, an altogether wilder affair. The Liard Hot Springs are located adjacent to one of the few campgrounds open year-round on the Alaska Highway. Instead of hotels and shops, campers and tired drivers will find the pool via a raised wooden boardwalk that crosses over a swamp.

Wildlife is known to gather from the surrounding boreal forest, and it's not uncommon to spot a moose here. You'll want to make

Top 10 Hot Springs in Western Canada

The region has just the right geological foundation for hot springs to flourish. Enjoy a soak in:

1. Liard Hot Springs, BC
2. Harrison Hot Springs, BC
3. Miette Hot Spring, AB
4. Ainsworth Hot Springs, BC
5. Radium Hot Springs, BC
6. Banff Upper Hot Springs, AB
7. Hot Springs Cove, BC
8. Temple Garden Mineral Spa, SK
9. Nakusp Hot Springs, BC
10. Halcyon Hot Springs, BC

some noise to let the bears know you're around, too. Once you arrive at the gravel-bottom pool, slip on your bathers in the change room and deposit your towel in a cubbyhole. Stairs lead you down into the spring, where temperatures range between 42°C and 52°C, depending where you sit (the stairs on the left lead to cooler water). Breathe. Soak. These rugged springs are absent of shops and tour buses and hordes of kids contributing to the liquid warmth. For its natural charm and therapeutic benefits on mind, body, and soul, Liard Hot Springs soaks its way into our bucket list.

START HERE: canadianbucketlist.com/liardhotsprings

BRITISH COLUMBIA ↑

STROLL THE SEAWALL

"Can you imagine, some people actually live here!"
I overheard that comment from one of the eight million
people who visit Vancouver's Stanley Park every year, during my first
stroll along its 8.8-kilometre paved seawall. When the sun is beaming, the park, and the city, has that effect on people. It's the first place
I take visitors to the city, the first and most powerful impression I
can give them. One second we're surrounded by apartment buildings, and the next we're in a tranquil forest, with stellar views of the
North Shore mountains, or the sun reflecting off the glass of buildings downtown. If you look at the view of downtown and Stanley Park
from across the Burrard Inlet on Spanish Banks, Stanley Park looks
almost exactly the same size as downtown, a perfect balance of nature
and city. With a half-million trees, two hundred kilometres of trails,
and attractions such as the world-class aquarium, some of the city's

Sea Vancouver

Vancouver joins Cape Town, Sydney, and Rio de Janeiro as one of the world's most beautiful cities. If you don't want to walk around Stanley Park, you can take a hop-on hop-off bus, harbour cruise, floatplane flight, or visit the Vancouver Lookout Tower. If you don't mind being out in the elements, I recommend Sea Vancouver's Zodiac tour. Well-priced, with the fun bonus of bouncing over waves, the ninety-minute ride covers Coal Harbour, English Bay, False Creek, and Stanley Park. Weatherproof cruiser suits are provided, but wear layers for the wind. ➤

START HERE: canadianbucketlist.com/seavancouver

Flyover Canada

Want to fly but afraid of heights? Vancouver's Flyover Canada is a fear-friendly simulation ride that puts you at the centre of a huge screen dome. Safely strapped into your chair, the floor drops away, and soon you're whoosh-ing through the Rockies, over cowboys in the Prairies, coastal rainforest, and into Niagara Falls. Engaging the rest of your senses, this "4D" eight-minute ride allows you to smell the scents and feel the mist and the wind. It's delightfully overwhelming; after all, Canada's beauty is nothing to scoff at.

START HERE: canadianbucketlist.com/flyover

The Wind Bomb

In December 2006, a powerful windstorm blew in from the Pacific, flattening forty-one hectares of Stanley Park forest and damaging Vancouver's beloved seawall. Aided by public donations and scores of volunteers, $10 million was invested planting fifteen thousand new trees and shrubs, rebuilding parts of the wall, upgrading the road, and improving park trails. The park's famous Hollow Tree was restored with a $100,000 private donation (and concealed steel pipes). ➤

best beaches, manicured gardens, Pitch n Putt, and concerts under the stars in Malkin Bowl, there's plenty to do in Stanley Park. Some might argue — under their voices during hockey season — that this is Lord Stanley's greatest legacy.

For our bucket list, simply walk or pedal around the seawall, taking in the views of mountains, city, ocean, birds, people. It's something to appreciate in all weather, but on a warm summer day it will probably make you want to live here, too.

START HERE: canadianbucketlist.com/stanleypark

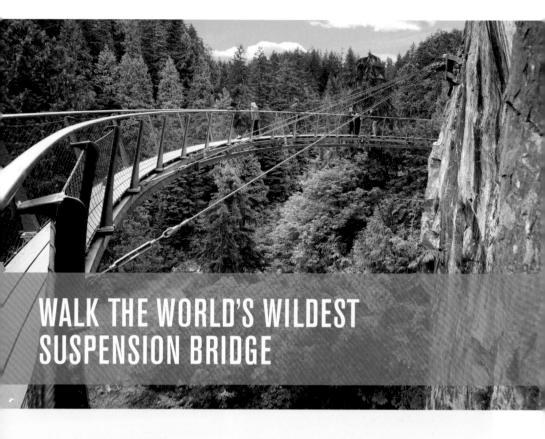

WALK THE WORLD'S WILDEST SUSPENSION BRIDGE

The Facebook post read: "13 Breathtaking Places Guaranteed To Make Your Stomach Drop." It's a typical headline you'll see these days in the frenzy of social media, although at least it wasn't accompanied by "It blew my mind" or "#5 made me laugh so hard I peed my pants." Naturally, I clicked on the link, where I found images from truly scary spots in Norway, China, Zimbabwe, and Spain, many of which I'd been to. But it was Number 10 on the list that stood out for me, for one very simple reason: it's one of the most popular and accessible tourist attractions in Vancouver.

Stretching 137 metres across North Vancouver's Capilano Canyon, the Capilano Suspension Bridge was originally built of hemp rope and cedar planks way back in 1889. Since then, it has

been completely reconstructed as the centrepiece of a West Coast outdoor eco-tourist theme park, which includes a treetop platform path built amidst 1,300-year-old Douglas fir trees, traditional totem poles, forest hikes, interpretation stations, and a series of cantilevered and suspended walkways constructed against a striking granite cliff.

Still, it's the suspension bridge that has attracted visitors for more than a century, swaying with every step, seventy metres above the Capilano River. Technically, there are longer suspension bridges that are not as high and higher bridges that are not as long. But few bridges are run like this slick tourism operation, with its heavy tour-bus traffic in the summer. Personally, I love the cool, clear nights of winter, when the bridge and treetop walkways are illuminated with Christmas lights, creating an experience that is just magical. Not that it needed the boost, but now that the Capilano Suspension Bridge has gone viral on social media, it's certain to remain on bucket lists for generations to come.

START HERE: canadianbucketlist.com/capilano

TASTE THE OKANAGAN

I'm on an electric-assist bike scooting alongside vineyards, the wind in my hair. It's a honeymoon of sorts, but since my wife and I cannot afford jet-setting to Tuscany, we drove four hours from Vancouver into the B.C. interior for our very own Canadian wine adventure. Certainly, there is nothing in Tuscany that remotely resembles the sparkling 135-kilometre-long Lake Okanagan. Neither do Tuscan wines benefit from the "lake effect" — a cooling of the temperature caused by the lake's deepness. Wines in the Okanagan's Lake County more accurately resemble those produced along the Rhine in Germany. Yet, as in all great wine regions, the caramel-coloured countryside here has the fragrance of a farmers' market. Summers in the Okanagan routinely bake the landscape above 40°C. And while the rest of Canada deals with harsh nine-month winters, Okanagan summers last from April to October. This might explain why the

Wine in B.C.

British Columbia produces over sixty types of varietals, the most popular reds being Merlot, Pinot Noir, and Cabernet Sauvignon, and the most popular whites Pinot Gris, Chardonnay, and Gewürztraminer. The province boasts five wine regions: Okanagan Valley, Similkameen Valley, Fraser Valley, Vancouver Island, and the Gulf Islands. ➤

region's largest city, Kelowna, has become one of the fastest-growing cities in North America, attracting everyone from tech start-ups to celebrity chefs.

Visiting over the years, I've always been surprised by just how beautiful this part of the world is, and how good the wine can be. A sommelier at Mission Hill, the region's biggest vineyard, tells me that the enjoyment of wine is all about context: where you are, how you feel, and whom you're with. Years earlier, I romanced a girlfriend in the Okanagan by visiting wineries in the back of an immaculately restored apple green 1953 Cadillac convertible. It was one of a hundred classic cars owned by Garnet Nixdorf, who offers chauffeured tours to vineyards around Penticton. Talk about context!

There are more than 120 wineries in the Okanagan, many opening their doors for summer tastings, with patio restaurants and artisan stores. Everyone has their favourites: Gray Monk, Burrowing Owl, Summerhill, Cedar Creek, Sumac Ridge, Dirty Laundry, Red Rooster, the rock 'n' rollers at Ex Nihilo. Wine is a taste to be acquired, and the Okanagan provides ample opportunity to do so.

While you're in the area, consider renting a houseboat to float on Lake Okanagan, complete with wet bar and Jacuzzi. On a sweet summer day, lounge on the thick carpet of grass below Mission Hill's watchtower with a chilled glass of white wine. It's balm for the soul. And a lot cheaper than flying to Italy.

START HERE: canadianbucketlist.com/okanagan

BRITISH COLUMBIA ↑

SEE THE SOCKEYE RUN ON THE ADAM'S RIVER

Every year, Pacific sockeye salmon swim up from the ocean into the very rivers and tributaries where they were once hatched. Then they proceed to find a mate, spawn, and die. Millions of them — even more during the dominant run, which takes place every four years.

Given the large numbers, it's worth noting that each female salmon will lay about four thousand eggs, of which only two will survive to fulfill the promise of this remarkable migration. Once the breeding is complete, the salmon's bright red spawning colour will fade to grey and, with their strength exhausted, the fish will

die and float downriver. You could snorkel with the salmon on Vancouver Island [see page 29], but if you prefer to stay dry, you can still experience this amazing natural phenomenon up close. Each Thanksgiving, as many as 250,000 people visit the Salute the Sockeye Festival on the Adams River, located about a one-hour drive from Kamloops. The crowds are here to see the world's largest return of sockeye salmon to a single river: a migration of people, drawn to the migration of a species that people love to eat.

Highway 5 (a.k.a. the Coquihalla, a.k.a. the Yellowhead Highway) is one of those drives you don't forget in a hurry. The scenery east of Hope is simply staggering (especially in the mountains of Coquihalla Pass, and most notably in the fall). With good weather and multiple lanes, it takes me less than four hours to drive from Vancouver to Kamloops, where I immediately stop in at one of my favourite brew pubs in the province, the Noble Pig Brewhouse.

One basket of crispy fried pickles and several more flights of beer later, I feel suitably inspired for a round of foot golf at the Sun Rivers Golf Course. Yes, foot golf is a real thing, as are the muscular big horned sheep who roam this scenic 18-hole course overlooking the city. Talk about natural hazards: I dribbled past a birdie and saw an eagle, but that's just par for the course.

But I came for the salmon, and to the salmon is where I shall go. So I wake up early the following morning to begin my drive along the Trans-Canada toward Jasper, turning off in the direction of Roderick Haig-Brown Provincial Park. Traffic is already lining the streets, so I keep going until I reach Shuswap Lake Provincial Park, where I meet up with Barb from Shuswap Unique Adventure Tours.

Barb leads off-road Segway tours into both provincial parks, and if you've never zipped around on a Segway, trust me, the best way to do it is among fall foliage, alongside a sparkling lake, and through leafy tree tunnels.

Barb provides me with some invaluable local information for viewing the blood-red salmon in their mating death throes. To see the fish clearly, polarized sunglasses are a must. Also, don't worry; everyone is struggling to take good photos. Having a polarized camera lens helps, or you could join the keeners, some of whom have travelled from as far away as Europe to don expensive wetsuits and underwater cameras. Despite the crowds, it's a lovely stroll along the riverbank, with plenty of space for everyone, and no shortage of salmon to observe.

Sockeye endurance is remarkable, but that doesn't stop me from craving some wild cedar-planked salmon when we return to the city. I feel terrible, but they *are* delicious, and humans *are* one of the two hundred species that rely on the annual runs. All in, it is a rather unique natural experience for a sunny fall weekend. Even better if you can visit during the week and avoid the crowded parking lot.

START HERE: canadianbucketlist.com/sockeye

FIND YOUR INNER OUTLAW
IN THE B.C. INTERIOR

I was not born to be wild. Never listened to heavy metal, thunder ter-
rifies me, and any attempt to grow a goatee yields an unkempt weed
patch. Although I've got my motorcycle licence, I've only rode a real bike
a couple of times (scooters don't count). Yet cruising a Harley Davidson
on the world's most scenic roads feels right for a Bucket List. As my car
heaves up the Coquihalla Pass from Vancouver to Kamloops, questions
cloud my mind like lines on a paisley bandana. Of all bikes, why am I
drawn to the loud, obnoxious one? What do the roads of the B.C. interior offer that others do not? Am I going to kill myself with a growling
1690cc air-cooled, twin-cam engine, with steel laced wheels and less
fuel economy than a Fiat 500? Is this an experience that belongs on the
Western Canada Bucket List? Questions, and no shortage of nerves, too.

Few machines inspire emotional attachment like a Harley. In the
lobby of the Kamloops Sheraton hotel, a rider shows me the serial
number of his first bike, which he has tattooed across his arm. It's the

weekend of the annual B.C. Poker Run, which attracts 750 Harley bikers from across the province. I expect to see aggressive bearded gangsters, tattoos, leather, bad teeth, and chains. Yet when I gaze across the Valleyview Arena, where bikers have gathered for a muscular dystrophy fundraising event, I instantly recognize this crowd: Bucket Listers — people of all shapes, colours, and income brackets, drawn to a dream and the promise of a Harley Davidson. It's the promise of renegade freedom, delivered with every throttle; the promise that lets imaginary urban outlaws ride into town on powerful steel horses. Wanted … not dead or alive, but back in the office on Monday morning.

Eagle Rider Kamloops rents Harleys by the day or week, while the town's tourism board has handily created five road trip itineraries showcasing the back roads and attractions of the B.C. interior. It's an attractive package that demands investigation, even if my previous hog was a tin-can scooter, one I mangled in a bike accident ten years

ago. That accident led directly to my career as a travel writer, so who knows where this bike will take me?

"Is this guy for real?" asks Eagle Rider's sassy rental manager. As soon as she hands me my black leather jacket and lets me pick out my choice of bike, my excitement accelerates. Straddling a Heritage Softail, it's difficult not to buy into Harley's visceral connection to danger. My eyes squint, my beard grows. With my extremely limited bike experience, I expected a raging bull I'd have to throttle under control. Instead, the Softail is simple to operate, stable, and incredibly forgiving. Japanese bikes might have more bells, whistles, and reliability, but Japanese bikes don't inspire delusions of rebellious grandeur. Plus we're in pioneer country, pockmarked with copper mines and ghost towns. The right kinda bike is calling for the right kinda road.

"B.C.'s interior has some of the most curvaceous roads in Canada," explains James Nixon, an editor at *Cycle Canada* magazine. "The East Coast is a close second, but B.C.'s roads are in better condition, and you can't beat the scenery." James has rented a Road King for the week, but is devoted to his BMW back in Toronto. "Harleys want to conquer riders' hearts," he explains, "but it's not always the bike that succeeds, it's the ride itself."

Kamloops is one of Canada's sunniest cities, boasting more parks than any other city in the province. Straddling the Thompson River, it has an average temperature of 27°C all summer, and is surrounded by scenic

Spot This Spotted Lake

Everyone loves a weird natural phenomenon. Northeast of Osoyoos on Highway 3, look out for the bizarre coloured pools of Spotted Lake. Sacred to the Okanagan First People, the mineral-rich spots are the result of evaporation (Osoyoos is one of the hottest and driest places in Canada). Since the lake sits on private property, pull your car or bike over for a photo from the gate. ➤

hills and valleys. It's a perfect launch pad for a road trip, even when an unseasonal storm blows in. I see lightning strike the valley below, which seems appropriate as I blaze out toward the Clearwater Corridor. I notice plenty of bikers on the road, passing each other with a casual wave, the camaraderie signal motorists never see. The highway meanders through rolling countryside, with traffic enjoyably light. After a couple of hours, I arrive at Helmcken Falls inside Wells Gray Provincial Park — a magnificent waterfall that deserves its own entry on our bucket list. Fuelling up before Highway 24, the same route fur traders used centuries ago, I cross into the Cariboo-Chilcotin region of British Columbia. Mirror lakes reflect the moody sky, my engine roars in fifth gear, a blustery wind slams against my leather armour. It's only the start of a five-day road trip, but bliss has found me early.

Bikers may look rough, but bucket list bikers shouldn't rough it. I didn't expect to find authentic Italian cuisine at the rustic Lac des Roches Resort, but here it is, al dente. The route turns south onto the twisty twin-lane blacktop of Highway 97, past the impressive Painted Chasm, and on to the towns of Clinton and Ashcroft. I roar alongside the Highland Copper Valley Mine, the largest open-pit copper mine in the country, continuing south toward Merritt and the historic Quilchena Hotel. The Softail is opening up to me, revealing her secrets. She's most comfortable at ninety to one hundred kilometres per hour,

but even on a steep uphill she's got plenty to give. And she gives it on Highway 5A, returning through Kamloops on my way to Lytton. If the Icefields Parkway (see page 116) is the world's most beautiful drive, then British Columbia's Highway 5A, together with Highway 33, must be among the most beautiful rides. On the bike, I smell the pine, taste the wind, and see the beauty of British Columbia's interior Salome, slowly peeling off her layers.

It can be difficult to know what we don't experience. What I thought was an outlaw, crime-soaked subculture is actually the domain of the pleasantly normal, give or take a few fermented apples. With my limited experience on a bike, what I expected to be dangerous was perfectly safe, provided I took it easy, employed common sense, and used the right gear. Harleys, I discovered, are much like their riders — seasoned, full of character, and more bark than bite. Kamloops proved an ideal gateway to explore the natural beauty of B.C.'s Thompson-Okanagan and Cariboo-Chilcotin Coast, and a rented Harley was the ideal vehicle from which to do it. Cars will do just fine, too, as will bicycles and RVs. This is bucket list country. Whatever revs your engine, go for it.

START HERE: canadianbucketlist.com/interior

LET IT HANG OUT ON WRECK BEACH

For all its natural wealth, Vancouver still has a reputation as a city allergic to fun. Transplants will be quick to tell you how polite yet unwelcoming the city can be, how rules and regulations suffocate events, and how the orchard of civic spirit is chopped down by City Hall in case of that one bad apple. And then you get Wreck

Beach. It gravitates on the city's most westerly point like antimatter, like anti-Vancouver. To get there, you must journey to UBC (the University of British Columbia), find parking, and walk down the 473 stairs of Trail Six as exhausted people pass you on the way up. At the bottom, you'll notice two things: a beautiful beach, and a motley collection of naked people.

Wreck Beach is clothing optional, but it is more than that. It's a community, dedicated to keeping the beach clean, the conduct becoming, and the creeps out. While it's impossible to buy food on the sand of any other beach in the city, here you can pick up a cold beer, a pizza, a bison burger, a veggie wrap, and even a cocktail from enterprising and spritely vendors in the buff. Kids run amok, safely observed by their parents and friends. Groups gather around logs, playing guitar and Frisbee, reading the paper or debating politics. Smell the tang of marijuana in the air, hear the beat of a drum, and be surprised that the majority of bodies belong to the weathered and

Nudity in Canada

Canadian law states it is unlawful to be nude in public, or dressed in a way that offends public decency. That includes you, Justin Bieber. Fortunately, there are places where we can run around in the buff, such as municipally approved clothing-optional beaches, and any place where nobody cares to call the authorities. Toronto's Hanlan's Point joins Wreck Beach as an official clothing-optional beach, while nudists gather unofficially at Crystal Crescent Beach (Halifax), in Oka Park (Quebec), and at naturist resorts around the country. ➤

leathered, not the rebelliously young. It can get really busy on sunny weekends, and increasingly tourists are finding their way here too.

Yes, City Hall, some people cannot hold their liquor and shouldn't be allowed to toke on the beach. But the vast majority of Wreckers are quite capable of looking after themselves, and deal responsibly with someone who steps out of line. When the police raid, as they seem to do more frequently, word rolls up along the beach to help everyone avoid a violation fine. They're just doing their jobs, but I've seen officers handle a wayward beer with far too much aggression, rightly earning a "shame on you" from nearby students and grandmas. Wreck Beach may not be everyone's cup of chai, and not everyone deserves all the freedom that it offers. Yet here is proof that beautiful Vancouver can let its hair down and bask in the sun without burning down the house. Have fun responsibly, and don't forget to apply sunscreen. Yes, there too.

START HERE: canadianbucketlist.com/wreck

CLIMB A MOUNTAIN WITH NO EXPERIENCE

Here's what we like about mountain climbing: the epic views, the physical challenge, the pristine mountain wilderness. Here's what we don't like about mountain climbing: the danger of slipping, falling, and dying, or worse, having to use a penknife to cut a trapped arm off. Fortunately, there's a place to meet in the middle. A *via ferrata* (Italian for "iron road") is a secure climbing route that allows you to clip safely into staples hammered into the rock, using your carabiner and harness to get to spots even traditional climbers can appreciate. Originally developed in the Alps to help soldiers scale mountains, *via ferratas* have become increasingly popular in mountainous regions, and British Columbia is no exception. The longest *via ferrata* in North America is CMH Summer Adventure's Mount Nimbus summit, accessible for guests at its helicopter fly-in, Bobby Burns Lodge. As you scale a sheer rock face along the spine

More Via for Your Rata

If you're lacking the daring (or more likely budget) to attempt Mount Nimbus, there are other options. Consider the four-hour *via ferrata* adventure to the top of Whistler Mountain, open to everyone over fourteen years of age. Banff National Park now has its own three-hundred-metre *via ferrata* above the Cliffhouse Bistro on Mount Norquay. Custom Outdoor Adventures operate a *via ferrata* on the 182-metre rock face between Nordegg and the Icefields Parkway, open to everyone ten years old and up. ➤

of the mountain, relax knowing that the iron rung ladders and sixty-metre-long rope suspension bridge are designed to take ten times the amount of weight you're putting on them. Relax knowing you're in the perfectly capable hands of expert guides and high-level gear. Relax knowing ... oh who are we kidding? Just because you're perfectly safe clinging to the rock face a thousand metres above the ground, doesn't mean you won't be quaking with fear. Still, one step in front of the next, and before you know it, you will be king (or queen) of the world. CMH, which runs eleven heli-ski lodges in the winter (see page 42), have another *via ferrata* near its Bugaboos Lodge called the Skyladder. Once again, the views are extraordinary, and hey, even your teenage kids can do it.

START HERE: canadianbucketlist.com/mountnimbus

FLOAT THE PENTICTON RIVER CHANNEL

Many years ago, I spent an afternoon floating on a rubber tube down the Mekong River in Laos, toasting my fellow floaters with cold Beer Lao, waving to locals on the riverbank, and celebrating my good fortune at having discovered such an activity in the first place. I thought I'd have to return to Vangvieng for that simple pleasure, until I saw the river channel linking Lake Okanagan and Skaha Lake in Penticton. Rubber tubes were floating down the canal

like twirling Froot Loops in a bowl of cherry cola. Every summer, the seven-kilometre channel fills with locals and visitors. Gliding on your back in the sun, a clandestine bottle of wine chilling at your side, you can take three to four hours to float the entire length, where a handy shuttle service awaits to return you to the entrance parking. Any inner tube, air mattress, raft, or floating device will suffice, available at stores around town or for rent from the shuttle service. The water is shallow and safe, with a halfway point to exit in case the sun is a bit much or the weather turns.

The river channel makes it onto the Bucket List for several reasons: First: this is not a water park but the fortunate by-product of a dredge built to control flooding in the 1950s. Second: It's relaxing as hell, free as air, and can be as social or meditative as you wish. (If you're lumped with a loud group of spotty teenagers, pull to the side in the two-metre-deep water and give them some distance.) It may not be as exotic as the Mekong River, but the accommodation and dining choices in Penticton are much better, trust me.

START HERE: canadianbucketlist.com/tube

CLIMB THE GRIND, HIKE THE CHIEF

Vancouverites have a special place in their hearts for physical pursuits. These are people obsessed with the outdoors, since it's among the best cities in the country, weather-wise, in which to enjoy it. Despite the "granola with my yoga" reputation, Vancouver also offers more demanding physical challenges. Take the Grouse Grind, "Mother Nature's Stairmaster," running 853 metres up the side of Grouse Mountain over a distance of exactly 2.9 kilometres.

At some point in your life, you've been physically exhausted — leg muscles burning, sweat stinging your eyes, mind full of blame. Well done, you've just reached the soul-crushing quarter-way sign on the Grouse Grind. The Grind is a walk in the park, and by walk I mean slog, and by park I mean mountain. In front of and behind you, you'll see others stuck in the same elevator from hell, but not to worry, everyone is too polite to panic. What's more, many will be dressed in form-fitting stretchy pants, because the Grouse Grind is not only a natural workout, it's become an unlikely pick-up joint for yuppies hell-bent on maximizing the tone of their glutes.

Among the 100,000 people who undertake the Grind every year, count on seeing at least one of the following during your visit:

- A young parent seriously regretting the idea that doing the Grind with their toddler on their back would be fun.
- Asian tourists who heard about one of the city's most popular hikes and had no idea what they were getting into. Typically wearing Hello Kitty sandals.
- A hiker well into his or her seventies who seems to be having no trouble whatsoever.
- The despair when people reach the quarter-mark sign.
- Someone arriving at the sad realization that there's no view, and nowhere to go but up.

Regular Grinders time themselves, with the average being about ninety minutes, and the current record an astonishing 23 minutes 48 seconds. My personal best up the 2,830 uneven dirt stairs is fifty-five minutes, but to be fair, I was drunk and in the mood for self-loathing. The reward for your calorie-decimating workout is typically beer and nachos at the Grouse Mountain bar. Take off, put on. Fortunately, it's only ten dollars for the gondola ride down to the parking lot, where you'll find a mix of exhausted, sweaty hikers and tourists reaching for their noses. If a Vancouverite asks to take you on the Grind, be prepared for a physical gauntlet. Or lie, with the reliable excuse, "I've done it, just over an hour, isn't it a bitch of a hike, wow, once was enough!"

Alternatively, there's another climb that's just a fraction less admired by Vancouverites: the Stawamus Chief, or, simply and respectfully, the Chief. This giant granite monolith sits seven hundred metres above the Howe Sound, overlooking the town of Squamish on the Sea to Sky Highway between Vancouver and Whistler. World-renowned with climbers who scale its impressive rocky face, hikers and day walkers can go around the back and climb to the Chief's three summits, where they'll find a truly staggering view of the fjords and coastal mountains. The well-maintained trails can be rugged and steep, with handy iron chains and ladders adding to the sense of adventure. Pack a picnic for the top, and marvel at the beauty that stretches out in every direction. You don't even have to rough it. Opened in 2014, the Sea to Sky Gondola offers a restaurant, coffee shop, and an easy way down.

START HERE: canadianbucketlist.com/grind

The Sea to Sky Gondola

Hikers of the world, relax. Squamish's new $22-million Sea to Sky Gondola not only preserves the Chief hike, it opens up astounding views of Howe Sound, Sky Pilot Mountain, and the mighty Chief itself. The 849-metre-long gondola ride takes you right to the top of an adjacent mountain, where you'll find a sixty-five-metre-high suspension bridge and scenic walking loops, as well as new hiking and biking trails. Celebrate the commendable execution of one of British Columbia's latest attractions with a craft beer on the sunny patio of the Summit Lodge.

START HERE: canadianbucketlist.com/seatosky ➤

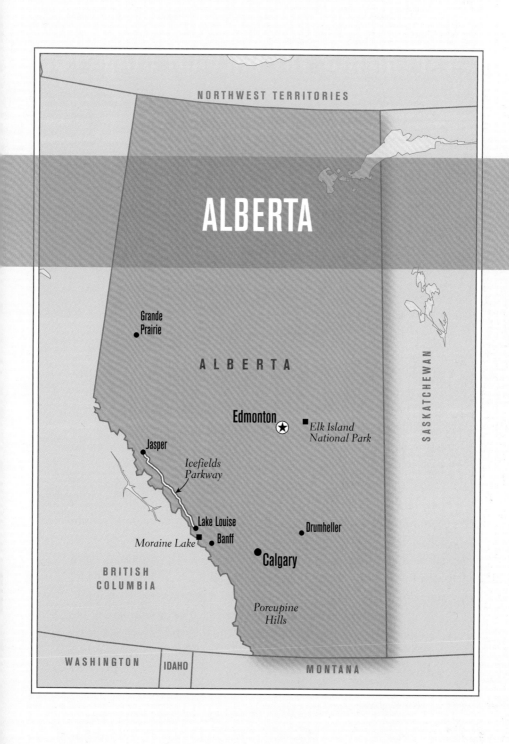

NORTHWEST TERRITORIES

ALBERTA

Grande
Prairie

ALBERTA

Edmonton ☆ ■ Elk Island
National Park

Jasper

Icefields
Parkway

Lake Louise
Moraine Lake Banff

Drumheller

Calgary

BRITISH
COLUMBIA

Porcupine
Hills

SASKATCHEWAN

WASHINGTON   IDAHO   MONTANA

EXPERIENCE THE CALGARY STAMPEDE

It may be many things to many people, but there's no denying the Calgary Stampede — that ten-day Cowtown spectacle — is something to experience before you die. For those who have been, or locals who live it, no explanation is necessary. For the rest of you, take it from a city slicker who came to love his inner yahoo, and to wear his white hat, buckle, and boots with pride. Here's why:

The festival attracts millions of people, from western Canada and beyond. Among them are party animals, herded through gates into wild nights at Cowboys, Nashville North, and other venues around town. They see the Stampede as an excuse to drink beer, dance on sticky floors, flirt with the opposite sex (in boots), perhaps go home with them, wake up, hate themselves, and repeat it all the following day. Strangely enough, older celebrants don't stray too far from the above, perhaps preferring smaller venues such as Ranchmans or bigger concerts like the Round Up. It's one of the world's biggest parties, if you're into that sort of thing, which the Stampede is more than willing to provide you an excuse to be.

Tips for a Stampede

1. If you don't have boots, get a pair at the Alberta Boot Company, which has been furnishing cowboys and their accountants for more than thirty years. That pain you feel breaking them in makes you a better person.
2. Pick up the traditional Calgary White Hat at Smithbilt, official hat maker for the event, and for the stars. Do not take it off, even when you sleep.
3. Never say *Yeehaw*. It's *Yahoo*. Remember that, or face a world of shame.
4. Line up for free bacon pancakes and festive chit-chat each morning at Flour Rope Square. Do not make fun of the clowns.
5. Win a prized item from China along the midway. Donate it to a kid, but not in a creepy sort of way.
6. Ride the abnormally fast Ferris wheel, pet an animal, visit the exhibitions, watch a miniature horse show, eat lunch in the Big 4, gear up for the rodeo.
7. Stay for the Big Show and fireworks.
8. After that, interact with local wildlife at Cowboys, Nashville North, or Ranchman's. ➤

Next, the Stampede is the World's Richest Rodeo. Before I understood exactly what the rodeo is, how it works, and who's behind it, I always rooted for bulls and horses. I'd yell at my TV set: *Throw that bastard off you and trample him in the mud!* I'm sure I'm not alone, but that changed when I decided to actually see what was going on for myself. Interviewing riders, judges, farmers, and vets, I found myself busting one rodeo myth after the next. No, the testicles of the animals are not strung up to make them buck. No, rodeo animals seldom get hurt and receive the best possible medical attention when they do. Yes, riders have the utmost respect for the animals, and bear the brunt of the injuries. No, the animals are never overworked, but are bred for their bucking ability, and live out their days like champions in the pasture. And yes, it's dangerous, as even a mechanical bull will snap your wrist. It's always difficult to lift a veil of assumptions, but having finally learned more about the rodeo, I see a timeless confrontation between man and beast, in fierce but relatively harmless battle, catering to and supported by the very people who work

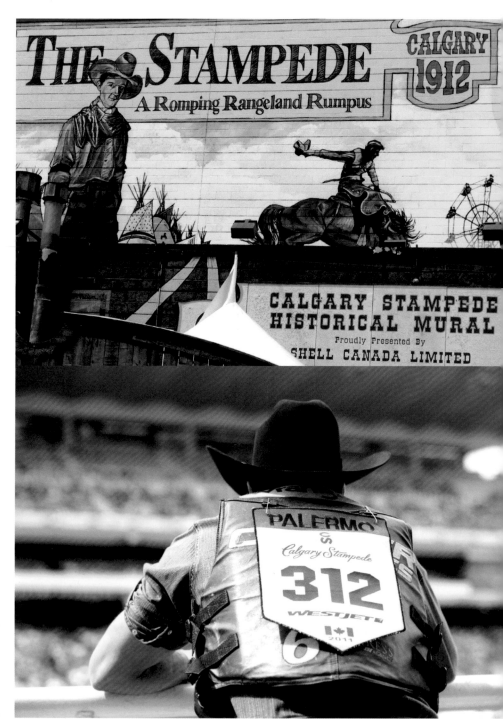

with animals in their daily lives. Animal rights activists may still want to string me up by my testicles, but I'll say this: go check out the rodeo, meet the people, see the animals, and form an educated opinion.

Finally, there's Cowtown itself: Calgary. Over the years I've visited the city during Stampede, and I'm always impressed with the community spirit behind the event. The free pancake breakfasts. The parades. The exhibitions. The Young Canadians. The performances. The volunteers who make the event tick, taking unpaid leave from work in order to do so. "Any time you can give back to the community, and help them out a little bit, you get something out of it," TV's Mantracker Terry Grant tells me. He's been a volunteer at the Stampede for years.

During my second Stampede, I was hell bent on breaking in a pair of boots and never left the hotel without my white hat. Before that, the only time I'd ever dressed like a cowboy was at Halloween parties, but here I can slot right in. Boots make me stand taller, puffing out my chest. The cowboy myth (see Ranch Vacation, page 110) still holds power in our modern age.

Certainly there are those who avoid the Stampede like a warm pile of cow droppings, but there's no denying the sheer energy that shakes up the city. Boots and hats are everywhere, kids have cotton-candy grins, the midway is buzzing. Like many items on the Canadian Bucket List, the Stampede is likely a saddle that fits some better than others. But as a true Canadian celebration of western roots and community spirit, you can't miss it.

START HERE: canadianbucketlist.com/stampede

ALBERTA ↑

SKI IN A UNESCO WORLD HERITAGE SITE

Canada has seventeen UNESCO World Heritage Sites, and it's safe to say that visiting them all should be on the National Bucket List. After all, these are places of unique physical and cultural significance worldwide. Still, a bucket list should transcend the thoughts of a committee, even if they get it right, and especially when they get it wrong. Some World Heritage Sites I've visited around the world consist of little more than historical rubble. Some sites are miss-them-if-you-blink-really-that-was-it? And some, like Banff National Park, are just so staggeringly gorgeous they belong in another category altogether.

In any season, the Canadian Rockies is the picture postcard of Canada. Vast carpets of forest, gemstone lakes, and mountains with views waiting to kick you in the plexus. It took genius, and considerable Canadian elbow grease, to set up three different ski resorts in the park: Lake Louise, Sunshine, and Norquay. Come winter, you can literally slide down the wilderness that surrounds you.

Lake Louise, the third-biggest ski resort in Canada, is View Central. Enjoying the resort's runs, I often had to stop and plop my butt in the snow simply to admire the vista. I was determined to hit every lift in one day, which I did, and was not disappointed. Thanks to its location inside a national park, respect for the environment takes precedence over the ambitions of a leisure corporation. Perhaps this is why Lake Louise is owned by one family, with patriarch Charlie Locke being the first guy to scale all ten peaks in the area. Here is a mountain for people who love mountains: million-dollar views, not million-dollar condos.

Closer to Banff town centre is Sunshine, a smaller resort famed for its champagne powder. Staying at the Sunshine Mountain Lodge, Banff's only ski-in, ski-out boutique lodge, it's easy to awake each morning to catch "first chair" and reap the rewards. For skiers and snowboarders, simply catching first chair is one for the bucket list, anywhere, especially with a dozen centimetres of fresh snow on the ground. Sunshine has the kind of snow that makes your skis smile. This from a guy who grew up in Africa, who first saw snow as a six-year-old during a freak storm in Johannesburg, and was told to hide under his school desk in case it was ash from nuclear fallout. True story.

For all the snow in Canada, and the resorts that offer world-class conditions without even trying, what's the big deal about the UNESCO designation? You probably won't ski among moose and elk (although one instructor tells me his girlfriend once saw a wolverine). Sunshine, Norquay, and Lake Louise — the Big Three, as they co-market themselves — look like typical resorts, with lifts and quads and young Australians sweeping chairs in exchange for a season pass.

Canada's UNESCO World Heritage Sites

1. Head-Smashed-In Buffalo Jump, AB
2. Historic District of Old Quebec, QC
3. Landscape of Grand Pré, NS
4. L'Anse aux Meadows National Historic Site, NL
5. Old Town Lunenburg, NS
6. Rideau Canal, ON
7. SGang Gwaay, BC
8. Canadian Rocky Mountain Parks, AB
9. Dinosaur Provincial Park, AB
10. Gros Morne National Park, NL
11. Joggins Fossil Cliffs, NS
12. Kluane / Wrangell–St. Elias / Glacier Bay / Tatshenshini, NT
13. Miguasha National Park, QC
14. Nahanni National Park, NT
15. Waterton Glacier International Peace Park, AB
16. Wood Buffalo National Park, NT/AB
17. Red Bay Basque Whaling Station, NL

There are après-ski bars serving craft beer and knee-high plates of nachos. So how is this different, you may ask? It could be the views from the chairs at Lake Louise. It could be the snow at Sunshine. It could be the homeyness of Norquay. It could even be the proximity of iconic and grand Canadian hotels: Fairmont's Banff Springs and Château Lake Louise. On investigation, I can confirm it's all of the above, wrapped in a shell of deep respect for its surroundings — safe, protected, but available to be enjoyed.

START HERE: canadianbucketlist.com/skibig3

ALBERTA ↑

HUNT FOR DINOSAURS

Oh, what irony that the fiercest creatures ever to roam the planet have been unearthed, literally, in Canada. Here, in the land where the mighty *Tyrannosaurus rex* roared, we now honour the beaver. *T. rex* would use beavers as tennis balls — assuming dinosaurs played tennis or coexisted with beavers. Regardless, their old bones, discovered in southern Alberta's Badlands, have been found in the world's richest fossil bed.

Like most young boys, I was fascinated by dinosaurs, reciting their long-winded -*saurus* names and taking extra time to look at today's tiny lizards, wondering where it all went wrong. Or, given the rise of mammals, right. Unfortunately, by the time I arrived at Dinosaur Provincial Park, I was just another jaded adult too consumed by maturity to appreciate the fact that I had just plucked a seventy-million-year-old dinosaur bone directly from the ground. The kids around me, however, went berserk.

ON THE BUCKET LIST: Professor Philip J. Currie

The world's foremost dinosaur expert (think Sam Neill in Jurassic Park, *who was partially based on Dr. Currie) digs into the National Bucket List:*

The Milk River Canyon north of the American border is Alberta's deepest canyon and is also in the most sparsely populated region in the southern half of the province. The unhindered view of prairie grasslands is augmented by a great bowl-like depression that slopes down toward the canyon, offering a spectacular view of the mysterious Sweetgrass Hills on the south side of the border. The Badlands have produced some of the most interesting fossils from the province, including embryonic duckbilled dinosaurs within eggs and a superbly preserved skeleton of the ancestor of *Tyrannosaurus rex*!

Professor Philip J. Currie,
World-renowned palaeontologist
Founder, Royal Tyrrell Museum of Palaeontology

All it takes is a little imagination. Seventy-five million years ago, the Red Deer River valley was as lush and tropical as Central America. Huge beasts roamed about, looking very much like giant lizards, or birds, or museum skeletons, depending on which theory you choose to believe in. When the dinosaurs woke up to the Worst Day Ever, and promptly died, their bones settled on the riverbed, were covered by soft sandstone and mudstone, and were all but forgotten until the 1800s, when the fiercest creatures on Earth, humans, now wore funny hats. During the last ice age, a glacier had removed the top level of dirt, exposing hundreds of bones from more than forty types of dinosaurs, including Tyrannosauridae, Hypsilophodontidae, and Ankylosauria (you know, the ones with thick ankles).

Today, this UNESCO World Heritage Site is more than just Dinosaur Central. Sure, the visitor centre and interpretation drives are interesting, and you can drive a couple of hours to the Royal Tyrrell Museum of Palaeontology in Drumheller to see what the fossils look like cleaned up and bolted together. But it's the landscape itself that struck me, dare I say it, like a meteor.

The Badlands are so called because the soil makes this land terrible for farming but wonderful for filming science fiction. Cracked grey earth resembling the skin of an elephant is tightly wrapped around phallic rocks called hoodoos. Rattlesnakes shake among the riverside cottonwoods, while the much smaller descendants of dinosaurs fly overhead or bask in the sun. Taking it all in, it's hard not to appreciate the scale of our planet's history, and the palaeontological riches of Alberta.

A couple of years later, I find myself extracting an articulated bone from a fossil bed cut into a steep cliff, an hour outside Grande Prairie. I am almost one thousand kilometres north of the Badlands, at the site of yet another remarkable discovery. Here, among oil and gas platforms, lies one of the world's next-richest fossil beds, as palaeontologists from around the world work each summer in sun and rain to extract one fossil after another. The world's most famous dinosaur guy, Canada's own Professor Phil Currie, is spearheading the charge, complete with a $26-million namesake museum to house new-found treasures unearthed from the area.

Oil and gas beneath the earth have made Alberta Canada's richest province. Yet its earth continues to yield riches that give us profound insight into the past. Whether you're into history, museums, or just unusual scenery, join the hunt for dinosaurs in Alberta. At least before a meteor comes out of nowhere, causes a deep impact, blocks out the sun, wipes out life, and forces you, inconveniently, to wait another seventy million years for the opportunity.

START HERE: canadianbucketlist.com/dinosaur

HELI-YOGA IN THE ROCKIES

If you place the prefix "heli" in front of any other word, the result can only sound impossibly and incredibly cool. Heli-shopping! Heli-badminton! Heli-dating! We've already covered heli-skiing in B.C., so let's get creative as we climb aboard a whirlybird to witness one of the very best views one can possibly see: the peaks, spires, glaciers, lakes, and valleys of the snow-capped Rocky Mountains.

I'm Lululemoning my way into the mountains for an afternoon of Rockies Heli Tours' "heli-yoga." It's the perfect blend of Western Canada: the healthy lifestyle choices of British Columbia wrapped in the big ideas and money of Alberta. I meet my hatha yoga instructor, Martha McCallum, who is also a certified hiking guide, wildlife

ALBERTA ↑

biologist and wellness coach. Like most yoga teachers I've encountered, she speaks with a voice as soothing as lip balm, edging me on to find my centre and connect with the earth, or in this case the mountains. She's well aware of the irony of using jet fuel for an elevating mind-body exercise, but it does bring us closer to nature without having to build any roads or destroy any shrubs. It's also a lot easier than hiking with a yoga mat.

Travel writers use the adjective *breathtaking* with far too much gusto (myself included). Breathtaking is when someone punches you in the stomach, or you're about to bungee jump off a TV tower in Macao (trust me). The view of the Rockies from a helicopter is simply awful. As in "fills one with awe," like the word was originally intended. *Awesome* is only some awe, but here we're talking full, as in "to the brim." Our pilot banks through the canyons, glides over sharp peaks, hovers over bighorn sheep and a lone wolf that should probably make the sheep nervous. From above, I feel like a kid who has skipped all his vegetables and gone straight to dessert. With no long hikes to the top, heli-touring is instant gratification.

We land on a site called the Wedding Knoll (what, you've never been to a heli-wedding?), where Martha safely ushers us out with mats and a picnic basket. The helicopter takes off just as smoothly as it landed, and we are all alone, 2,700 metres up, embedded in wilderness. She lays out the mats, using rocks to keep them grounded in the mountain breeze, and begins the first pose. The goal of yoga is to meditate to a point of perfect mind-body tranquility. Usually this is done in a room with polished hardwood floors, mirrors, New Age music, and a dozen ladies wearing stretchy pants that flatter their buttocks. On the mountain, we still wear stretchy pants but have either far more or far fewer distractions, depending on your love for nature or for the behinds of yoga practitioners.

After the forty-five-minute class, we dine on Martha's homemade organic sandwiches and follow that up with a short heli-hike along the spine of the mountain. I decide that all hikes in the mountains

should start at the top and then just stay that way. Our helicopter returns, and the reward for this strenuous day of exercise is another fly-by through the mountains. *Namaste!*

It is certainly not essential to combine yoga with your heli-flight-seeing experience in the Rockies. Not all of us are in pursuit of mind-soul nirvana, and not all of us want to stretch into a pretzel. Seeing the Rocky Mountains from above, on the other hand, is a must. Heli-hiking, heli-poker, heli-cooking — just add the prefix *heli-* and you've got a winner, flying high on the Great Western Canada Bucket List.

START HERE: canadianbucketlist.com/heliyoga

HIKE THE SKY

Widely regarded as the best hike in the Rockies, over half of Jasper National Park's forty-four-kilometre Skyline Trail is above the treeline. Expect spectacular views as you cut across ridges that overlook crystal lakes, alpine meadows, and Tolkien-esque valleys. Be aware that hiking this high up also means greater exposure to the elements, particularly along Maligne Ridge, where strong wind and whipping rain can make life particularly miserable for trekkers. When in doubt, channel Frodo … he always kept going.

Depending on your level of fitness and sense of purpose, the Skyline Trail can be completed in anywhere from two to six days, and there are well-serviced campsites along the way. If you're lucky, you might see some of the animals that roam the high valleys looking for food, such as wolves, grizzly bears, and mountain lions. You'll feel even luckier if you're carrying bear spray.

Due to the unpredictable weather, you'll want to invest in quality gear, including a camping stove, since no fires are allowed on the trail. Tour companies in Jasper offer a shuttle service between the trailheads of Maligne Canyon and Maligne Lake, with most hikers choosing to start at the lake, avoiding a nasty early ascent. As one of the best-known hikes in the Rockies, booking ahead is essential. For those who would rather sit than walk, look into one of the horseback riding trips to the backcountry lodge that sits midway along the trail.

START HERE: canadianbucketlist.com/skyline

BE THE COWBOY ON A RANCH VACATION

Cowboys date back to the 1700s, the name being a direct translation of the Spanish *vaquero*, a person who managed cattle by horseback. Cattle drives, averaging around three thousand head, were managed by just ten men or fewer, each with several horses, battling the elements to literally drive the meat to market. The cowboy, often poorly paid, uneducated, and low on the social ladder, had many tasks to perform. These included rounding up the cattle; sorting, securing, and protecting herds from thieves and wild animals; breaking in horses; and birthing and nursing sick animals.

The hazardous and strenuous nature of the work created a breed of hardened men and terrific fodder for the romance novels eagerly snapped up by urban readers fascinated by the call of the Wild West.

Despite Hollywood's portrayal, there were relatively few violent confrontations with Native Americans. Instead, most Indian chiefs were paid in cattle or cash for permission to drive cattle through their lands. Another aspect glossed over in the folklore is that, according to the U.S. census of the time, 30 percent of all cowboys were of African or Mexican ancestry. Giddy-up amigo! When railways replaced cattle drives, modern cowboys began to work on ranches and show off their skills at competitive rodeos.

Our bucket list is now singing that old eighties song: "I Wanna Be a Cowboy." Who am I to argue?

Bill Moynihan talks with a throat of gravel, as if he's been chewing on the bones of Jack Palance and needs a can of oil to wash it down. He may be seventy-five years old, but the patriarch of the 120-acre Skyline Ranch is as tough and grizzled as any bootstrapping cowboy. Located in the Porcupine Hills, Skyline offers ranch vacations where guests can assist with daily chores, including feeding the three hundred head of cattle, roping up steers, and patrolling for wild animals. The area, captured beautifully in Ang Lee's *Brokeback Mountain*, sweeps up to the Rocky Mountains on the horizon. Bill's kids and grandkids are all involved in the family operation, a working ranch where you can leave your hat on and get your hands dirty.

Bill's moustache looks like an army guarding his upper lip. The former boxer, bush pilot, cop, and rodeo cowboy sizes me up. I'm a regular cowpoke, as alien to life on a ranch as I am to life in the Himalayas. I select a white horse named Barry (ahem) and saddle up for my first roundup. Here's what they don't tell you about Angus

ALBERTA ↑

Speak Like a Cowboy

Grab your bangtail from the picket line and hop in the rig, here's some genuine cowboy slang to prove you're not a city slicker (even if nobody will know what the heck you're talking about).

bake: When you ride your horse too hard, you bake it

bangtail: a mustang

burn the breeze: gallop at full speed

chewed gravel: got thrown from a horse

dusted: got thrown from a horse

grassed: got thrown from a horse (sense a theme?)

greenhorn: someone from the East who don't know diddly-squat

hurricane deck: what you sit in when a horse starts bucking

outlaw: a horse that cannot be broken

owl head: a horse that won't stop looking around

rig: a saddle

saddle bum: a drifter

slicker: a raincoat

widow maker: a misbehaving horse ➤

cows: they're big, and they can be rather belligerent. My cutting horse, bred for sudden stops and bucking cows, isn't fazed. Bill lassos a young calf and I assist with tagging it on the ear, nervous about its six-hundred-kilogram mom who seems endearingly protective. Next I feed heifers some grain and dispense hay from an industrial tractor. While I barely manage to heave a bale of hay to the shed, Bill walks past carrying two on each hand. When the zombies attack, I hope I'm around a guy like Bill.

Skyline guests can also go hiking, fishing, biking, and horse riding in the hills, but ranch work is where the action is. Moving hay, shovelling shit, feeding the animals: farm life is physically tough and yet satisfyingly simple. You know what has to be done, and you do it.

That evening, over cold cans of Lucky Lager, I share stories with Bill and his son Reid, learning about the respect one has for the environment when one actually lives in it. "When the stars are out, you can see just about every one of them," explains Reid, feeding the firepit. The chain bonding ranching and nature is thick, and the

Moynihans have a deep appreciation and respect for the animals and the land that provide their livelihood.

They also have a deep appreciation for fun. When Bill teaches me how to lasso, the only thing I succeed in lassoing is my eyeball. City slickers are always good for a laugh around the fire.

The following day, I succeed in sticking my arm deep inside a pregnant cow's vagina, verifying all is ripe for birthing. Yes, I've come a long way in a couple of days. We saddle up for a ride to the property fences, making sure nothing is damaged and looking for signs of predators. A strong, icy wind blows across the foothills.

"The biggest thing you can do in life is pass on the thing you love to somebody else," Bill tells me. He is not a man of many words, but cowboys don't have to be. I try to grunt, but it comes out like a squeak.

The word *dude* technically refers to someone who doesn't know cowboy culture but pretends otherwise. You can also refer to a dude as being "all hat and no cattle." A dude like, say, me. Yet the hospitality from these earthy folks was wonderfully warm and genuine, and the values of the modern-day cowboy seem to be alive and well. As it rides its way onto our Bucket List, ranch life remains as real and alluring as the cowboy myth that promotes it.

START HERE: canadianbucketlist.com/ranch

RV THE ICEFIELDS PARKWAY

The first time I hauled a backpack around the world, I had a wonderful sensation of independence. Everything I needed was right there: clothes, toiletries, my iPod, books, cash, a sense of adventure. My daily challenge was deciding where to sleep and use the toilet. The first time I went on an RV adventure, I felt that familiar gush of independence, only the daily challenges were flushed away with the black water.

My dad, my brothers, and I had rented a nine-metre Winnebago for a week's Mancation to the Rockies. We would become just one of over a million RVs on Canadian roads that summer, the others hopefully driven by people with more experience than us. With a complete kitchen, two television sets, a bedroom, and a bathroom, the RV rattled and rolled its way out of Vancouver, wobbling in the wind with the aerodynamics of a cement brick. I was driving, my brothers were yelling: "Too close to the side!" "Watch the lines!" "You almost hit that car!" Ah yes, just a few hours in and I could feel our Mancation easing my stress . . . right up behind my eyeballs and straight to the back of my throat.

My dad has always been in love with mountains, but since emigrating from South Africa he'd never had the opportunity to see the Rockies. For the full effect, I steered our roadworthy beast to Highway 93 — a.k.a. the Icefields Parkway — a 232-kilometre stretch of road between Lake Louise and Jasper. It is, without a doubt, one of the world's most spectacular drives, a gee-whiz postcard moment waiting for you at every turn. The visual impact of the mountains and glaciers that line the highway rivals that of the Himalayas, but boy, the Rockies are a lot easier to get to. Passing turquoise lakes and glacier-cut mountains, we craned our necks from side to side to capture the view out of the large windows, like we were watching a game of tennis. The overall effect, especially for someone who enjoys mountain beauty, can be as rich as overly cheesy fondue. "It's too much," I heard my dad reporting to my mom on his cellphone. "But in a good way."

Rock flour, crushed and carried by glaciers, makes mountain lakes glow in luminous shades of blue and green. We visit Moraine Lake on a postcard-perfect day, getting our group photo in front of one of Canada's most popular and sought-after views. By the time we reach Peyto Lake, farther up the highway, our camera batteries need refuelling from the RV's generator. The RV's height, big windows, and ease of movement made it the perfect vehicle from which to gawk at the mountains, if not always to park. Thank you, Parks Canada, for the extra-long parking bays at all the major sites. Parks Canada protects our wilderness, and they park Canada too!

Canada's Top RV Destinations

GO RVing is an organization representing RV dealers, manufacturers, and camp-ground operators that helps to promote the freedom, flexibility, and fun of the RV lifestyle. Here's a list from their Top Destinations to RV in Canada:

BC Ashnola River
      Bella Coola

AB Banff National Park
      Beauvais Lake Provincial Park/
      Waterton Lakes National Park

SK Douglas Provincial Park
      Duck Mountain Provincial Park

MB Spruce Woods Provincial Park

ON Algonquin Park
      Bronte Creek Provincial Park

QC Bannick, Ville-Marie
      Gaspésie

NS Aspy Bay, Cape Breton
      Cabot Trail

NB Fundy National Park
      Littoral Acadien

PEI Cavendish Sunset
      Twin Shores, Darnley

NL Gros Morne
      Twillingate

YK Kluane Lake
      Tatchun Lake

We pop into the Athabasca Glacier, where monster customized four-by-four buses take us directly onto a six-kilometre-long ice floe in the Columbia Icefields. Out on the ice, I scoop up melted water, drinking the taste of nature at its purest.

Bookending the Parkway are two of Canada's most iconic wilderness areas: Banff and Jasper national parks. No surprise that we came across a bear chewing berries alongside the road, or huge elk stopping traffic in its tracks. During the week, we take the Banff Gondola and the Jasper Tramway, barbecue

steaks in an RV park, play a terrific round of golf at the Jasper Park Lodge, rent Harley-Davidsons to rocket up Mount Edith Cavell, and even swim in the ice-cold waters of a glacial lake. It is, in short, an epic Mancation, immersed in true Canadiana. We even manage to keep the RV in relatively good shape, although on the last night of our journey we realize that nobody had been paying too much attention to the instructions about how to empty the black water. Push a few buttons, pull a few knobs, and the next thing we know, the tube comes loose and drenches my brother and me. Truth be told, black water looks rather yellow. My dad would have wet himself laughing, but of course we'd already beaten him to it.

I've been on the Icefields Parkway several times since, yet the RV trip stands out. Travel magic is not about what you're doing, it's about whom you're doing it with. Wise words to remember when crossing off any item on your Bucket List.

START HERE: canadianbucketlist.com/icefields

CANOE ON MORAINE LAKE

J ust fifteen minutes from Lake Louise can be found one of the most magnificent views in all of Canada. The jewels of the Rockies gather in one magical spot — dramatic snowcapped peaks, emerald evergreen forest, a turquoise lake, and an easy-to-access lookout point — sparkling together on a crown of natural beauty the entire nation can wear with pride.

It took less than a decade after its discovery in 1899 for tourists to start arriving at Lake Moraine, which was soon serviced by a teahouse, and later tents and log cabins. Today, visitors will find luxury accommodations in the form of the Arthur Erickson–designed Moraine Lake Lodge, which is open each summer.

After feasting in the restaurant on gourmet dishes, such as bison carpaccio and deer tenderloin, head down to the mirror-like glacier-fed lake to rent a canoe. On a sunny day, with the Valley of the Ten Peaks reflected in the water, you just might think you'd died and gone to heaven.

START HERE: canadianbucketlist.com/moraine

STEP OVER THE ROCKIES

Mind-blowing views: the Rocky Mountains, and the Icefields Parkway in particular, have no shortage of them. Yet there's always room for more, especially if we can add in the word *knee-shaking*. Inspired by the Grand Canyon Skywalk, the same folks behind the Columbia Icefield glacier tours spent $21 million to build a horseshoe-shaped glass-floor observation deck extending thirty-five metres over and three hundred metres above Jasper National Park's Sunwapta Valley. Opened in 2014, the Glacier Skywalk is another meaty mouthful of natural beauty in a region that won't stop dishing it out until you explode — or at least unbuckle your belt.

With the environmental blessing of Parks Canada, your experience begins at Brewster's Glacier Discovery Centre down the road. A shuttle departs every fifteen minutes from existing parking lot facilities, ensuring no additional paradise paving was necessary. The short bus ride is further symbolic since it was a company bus driver who originally conceived the idea of a suspension bridge across the valley. Architects did one better, creating the steel-and-glass structure that places you right into the view itself. First you must walk through six interpretative stations, revealing the natural history, ecology, wildlife, and geology of the area. Suitably informed, the giant glass horseshoe awaits.

ALBERTA

Glass is a funny thing. Even when it's reinforced, 3.81 inches thick, and capable of withstanding the weight of two Boeing 747s, it still seems woefully inadequate. Especially when you take your first steps off a cliff and see the ground disappear between your feet. Some people just don't do heights — be it bungee jumping or glass platform observation decks. I'd suggest they take the Columbia Icefields Tour while the rest of us walk nervously forward to the apex of the platform. Immediately apparent: the Skywalk jiggles slightly when you walk. Engineers designed the platform to withstand metres of heavy snow, and sway safely in strong valley winds. Suspended high above the valley floor, you'll eventually be able to tear your eyes (and cameras) away from your feet and look out at Mount Andromeda, the Snow Cone, and its surroundings. You might even spot a bighorn sheep on the valley floor below. Standing on that platform is a bucket list moment, one that some visitors will want to experience for as long as they can. Others will be more than happy to take a few pictures and return their feet to solid earth.

START HERE: canadianbucketlist.com/skywalk

VISIT AN OASIS OF WILDLIFE

North America's largest terrestrial mammal, the bison once roamed the plains in the millions. Indigenous people hunted the huge beasts for meat and skins, and there was more than enough to go around. The arrival of European hunters, however, quickly took the species to the brink of extinction. Today, wild bison are protected in enclaves of national parks, the most famous and certainly the largest being Wood Buffalo National Park.

Far more accessible, and just as significant, is Elk Island National Park, located an hour's drive east of Edmonton. The country's only entirely fenced national park, Elk Island is a haven for free-roaming bison, not to mention elk, deer, moose, and more than 250 species of birds. Here, Canada's largest mammal shares its habitat with Canada's smallest — the pygmy shrew.

By the year 1900, there were as few as 1,500 plains bison remaining. Early conservation efforts saw the establishment of Elk Island in 1906, with several hundred pure-bred plains bison shipped up from

Montana. Their numbers rebounded, with the park eventually successfully relocating bison throughout Canada, the United States, and even as far as Russia. Elk Island also contains the most genetically pure wood bison remaining, as the two species have interbred everywhere else. The two breeds are kept separate in the park, with wood bison on the south side of the Yellowhead Highway and plains bison on the north side. On either side, visitors can leave their cars to hike or hit the mountain biking trails in summer, and snowshoe or cross-country ski in winter. On these treks, it's not uncommon to encounter grazing bison herds and other wildlife. Today, there are more than eight hundred bison in the park, the number maintained so as not to overwhelm their sanctuary. Parks Canada's interpretation and conservation efforts are an encouraging sign that bison will remain a wildlife encounter on Western Canada Bucket Lists for many years to come.

START HERE: canadianbucketlist.com/elkisland

ALBERTA

HIT YOUR TARGET AT THE WEST EDMONTON MALL

Yes, I'm fully aware how this looks. Here's a book listing the ultimate things to do in western Canada before you die, and you just read: visit a mall. It's not even the biggest mall in the world. That honour belongs to — No, wait, someone else just built a bigger one. Yet Canadian malls are a little different. Take Montreal's Underground City. Officially called RÉSO, it's a warren of tunnels beneath twelve square kilometres of downtown Montreal, linking shops, hotels, residential buildings, schools, train and bus stations, offices, and tourists searching for a glimpse of daylight. Accessed by half a million people every day in winter, RÉSO contains several malls and so cannot technically be called a solitary mall in its own right. Calgary has its four-storey CORE, beneath three city blocks and with 160 stores. "Big deal!" yawn our friends in Ontario, where Toronto's Eaton Centre has 330 stores, Brampton's Bramalea City has

342, and Mississauga's Square One a whopping 360 places of commercial worship. In British Columbia, where people can actually step outside in winter, Burnaby's Metropolis at Metrotown trumps them all, at 450 stores, including a massive Asian supermarket.

Yes, Canadians like to shop, and by the looks of it, they like to shop at the same chain stores you'll find at just about every mall in the country. And then, suddenly, like an unexplained star burning across the retail sky, you get the phenomenon of the West Edmonton Mall. The largest mall in North America has over 800 stores, covering 570,000 square metres of retail, more than double the size of Metropolis. There's parking for more than 20,000 cars, it employs more than 20,000 people, receives 30 million visitors a year, and is Alberta's busiest tourist attraction.

I hear you asking: "Robin, seriously, isn't one mall just a carbon copy of the next? Stores, food court, gadget stores, teenagers in painted-on jeans, glass elevators, confusing maps?" I thought so, too, until I found myself pulling the trigger of a .44 Magnum revolver, blasting a bottle-cap hole in my paper target — at the West Edmonton Mall.

How many malls are accredited as a zoo? How many malls boast the world's second-largest indoor amusement park, complete with twenty-four feature rides and a thrilling roller coaster called the Mindbender? How many malls have the world's largest indoor water park, with the world's largest indoor wave pool, twenty-five-metre-high slides and a bungee jump tower? At this mall, you can say hello to the sea lion that swims beneath a replica of Señor Columbus's *Santa Maria*, skate on an Olympic-sized hockey rink, and then transplant yourself to New Orleans, Paris, or Beijing at one of three themed areas: Bourbon Street, Europa Boulevard, and Chinatown. Should you get tired of walking around trying to make sense of the thoughtfully provided maps, take a nap in one of the mall's two hotels.

You might expect to find such a mall in Vegas, or perhaps Dubai, which stole the Biggest Mall in the World title before relinquishing it to China, Malaysia, and the Philippines. Asian malls dominate the list

Canadians Are Shopaholics

According to a report by KPMG, nine of North America's fifteen most productive malls are in Canada. Measured by their sales per square foot, these include:

Sherway Gardens, Toronto ($950/sq. ft.),

Chinook Centre, Calgary ($1,055/sq. ft.),

Oakridge Centre, Vancouver ($1,200/sq. ft.),

Yorkdale Shopping Centre, Toronto ($1,300/sq. ft.),

Toronto Eaton Centre ($1,320/sq. ft.) and, topping the list, beating out Caesars Palace in Vegas ($1,470/sq. ft.) as the most productive mall on the entire continent: **Vancouver's Pacific Centre**, at a whopping $1,580/sq. ft. ➤

of biggest malls, but standing out like a proud beaver among the tigers is our very own West Edmonton Mall. To celebrate, I armed myself.

Flora Kupsch owns the family-friendly Wild West Shooting Centre. Flora is a multidisciplinary champion in firearms competitions and ably hands me a nine-millimetre .357 and a .44 Magnum bazooka. The Wild West sells a range of ammunition and guns, and offers various packages to clients who visit from all over the province. Where else can you pick up a bikini, do the groceries, and let off a few rounds? Increasingly, many of Flora's customers are young girls, strung out on *Twilight*, aiming for Team whoever they're not into that month.

I surprised Flora, and myself, by turning out to be a pretty good shot. Is there another mall where you can walk out with lingerie for your wife and used target sheets? Exactly.

START HERE: canadianbucketlist.com/wem

HIKE OR SKI INTO SKOKI LODGE

In 1931, Swiss mountain guides and members of the Banff Ski Club decided to build western Canada's first commercial ski lodge. With thousands of kilometres to choose from, they settled on a place called Skoki, selected for its scenic beauty, quality of snow, proximity to a creek, and safety from avalanches. Today, one of the oldest and highest backcountry lodges in Canada is an eleven-kilometre hike from the groomed ski slopes of the Lake Louise Resort, and I'm feeling every step of it.

It's my first time on cross-country skis, slipping and sliding forth with surprising ease. A strip of material under each ski, called the skin, grips the snow as I edge my way through pine forest, over frozen

The Royal Throne

When the newly married Duke and Duchess of Cambridge needed time alone on their first royal visit to Canada, Skoki Lodge was the perfect fit: miles away from the paparazzi, relaxing, and in the bosom of the Rockies. Skoki's staff worked with royal handlers to keep the destination mum and prepare it for the future King and Queen of England (and Canada). This meant the no-running-water, no-electricity charm of Skoki would need a little polish. A helicopter brought in a modern bathroom, complete with flush toilet, bathtub and sink, painstakingly installed to the bemusement of long-time staff, who have always found other ways to make do. Everything went off splendidly, even if the royal stay was less than twenty-four hours. As for the bathroom, it was hastily demolished and cleared away. Since Skoki is a wonderful slice of rustic history, guests are directed to the outhouses, as perfectly serviceable a throne as any. ➤

lakes, and across windy mountain passes. Every guest must ski, hike, or snowshoe in, unless you're the Duke and Duchess of Cambridge, in which case Parks Canada will organize a helicopter. Skoki made headlines for attracting the newly wed William and Kate on their Canadian honeymoon. No electricity, no cellphone or Internet coverage, no running water, no paparazzi — Skoki provided a rustic royal break from the media frenzy. It wasn't the first royal connection either: one of the lodge's first guests was one Lady Jean, a lady-in-waiting to Queen Victoria, who visited Skoki with her travel-writer husband, Niall Rankin. While the Rankins used the outhouse like regular guests, William and Kate had a specially built bathroom constructed for their visit, which was hastily destroyed afterward, lest regular guests get any ideas.

Skoki strives to be as authentic a backcountry experience today as it was in the 1930s. That means candles, blankets, and late-night stumbles to the outhouse during blizzards. It's one of the best winter adventures in North America, with an emphasis on adventure. You'll

know this as you make your way up Deception Pass, a steep uphill that keeps going, and going, and going. By the time I arrive, covered in sweat and snow from too many downhill tumbles, the fireplace is surrounded by guests enjoying hot homemade soup. The lodge accommodates up to twenty-two guests, and we each feel we deserve our place on one of the sink-in couches. Among the guests are two Norwegians, a ski club from Manitoba, a couple returning for the ninth time from the Northwest Territories, a birthday party, and a couple on their second honeymoon (staying in the Honeymoon Cabin, of course). Will and Kate, who signed the guest book like everyone else, preferred the Riverside Cabin, close to the creek. I offload my gear in a cabin called Wolverine, named for the wolverine that got stuck in it and almost tore it to shreds. Although Skoki's original builders took refuge in a special bear tree, the bears, cougars, and wolves that roam Banff National Park nowadays keep their distance. The most bothersome creatures appear to be pine martens, porcupines, and exhausted travel writers.

ALBERTA

Skoki itself is the launch pad for hiking and skiing trails, which most guests explore on their second day. Two-night stays are typical, giving you just about enough time to recover from the eleven-kilometre trek in order to do it all over again. Nobody can expect to lose much weight, however. The chef and staff somehow prepare gourmet meals, such as coconut-crusted Alaskan halibut, marinated tenderloin served with candied yams, avocado Caesar salad, and fresh homemade bread. That everything is packed in by snowmobile (horses in summer) and prepared using propane stoves makes it all the more impressive, and appreciated.

The discussion by the fire revolves mostly around Skoki's beauty, history, and legacy. One couple sifts through the guest books until they find the last time they signed it, in 1974. Another guest plays the piano, helicoptered in sometime in the early 1980s. I read an old book about western Canadian outlaws, play with Lucy and Bill (Skoki's resident Jack Russells), and let the fresh air and exercise sink into my pores. On my final night, the moon is so full I can read without a headlamp. Miles away from anything, protected by a world of mountains, forest, and snow, Skoki is the perfect escape, for royals and the rest of us.

START HERE: canadianbucketlist.com/skoki

VISIT A SITE FOR ALL EYES

The Rockies rock in all seasons, which is why you can't go wrong whenever you choose to visit. If it's warm and sunny, you hit the hikes. If it's cold and snowy, you ski the slopes. Or, in the case of Maligne Canyon, explore the ice. Despite the shadowy roots of its name (from the old French word for "evil"), Maligne is Jasper

ALBERTA

135

National Park's top-rated attraction. In the summer months, a river barrels through crevices in the limestone canyon, some as deep as fifty metres. This rush of water is best viewed from the well-trodden footpath and a series of six bridges, accessible via an easy two-hour round-trip walk with the welcome refreshment of pure glacier waterfall spray. Exit, as always, through the gift shop.

In winter, the gushing water freezes on the canyon floor, ideal for a guided ice-walk both alongside and through the canyon. Tour operators provide the cleats, headlamp, and interpretation of the canyon's unique topography (it sits above the largest karst cave system in North America). Candle-wax-like ice spikes cover the rocks. Walking among the crystals of the canyon's flash frozen waterfalls never fails to impress, nor does the site of water still flowing beneath the ice in some sections. Ice chutes create natural slides, which are particularly popular with the kids. They might want to break off an ice pick for an all-natural glacial ice-lolly — there's plenty to go around — and unlike stalactites, it won't take a thousand years to grow them back.

Whether you're chasing raging torrents, sparkling ice, or just the chance to immerse yourself in the beauty of one of Canada's most famous national parks, Maligne Canyon is a bucket list item for all seasons.

START HERE: canadianbucketlist.com/maligne

ALBERTA ↑

BOARD THE ROCKY MOUNTAINEER

All aboard for one of the world's great train experiences. I'm not talking about the time I spent thirty-eight hours in a cabin with slaughtered chickens in Zambia, with deafening music blasting through the cobwebbed, distorted speakers. No, the Rocky Mountaineer is an altogether more genteel affair, smothered in five-star service, tasty libations, and views of the Rockies in all their splendour. Running on four routes going both east and west, the Rocky Mountaineer is North America's largest private rail service. *National Geographic* called it one of the World's Greatest Trips, and *Condé Nast Traveler* listed it among the Top 5 Trains in the World.

I hopped on board at the station in Vancouver for a two-day journey up to Banff.

You don't sleep on the Rocky Mountaineer. The thousand-kilometre journey takes place during daylight so you can enjoy the views, with passengers staying overnight at the company's hotel in Kamloops. Guests are seated in a two-level, glass-domed coach with panoramic views, drinks service, and a helpful, unnervingly cheery attendant pointing out places of interest along the route. On the way out of B.C. we pass over Hells Gate, the narrowest point of the Fraser River, and spot a bear walking across the tracks behind us. We enter the engineering marvel of the Spiral Tunnels and are halfway through a game of cards when Mount Robson, the highest mountain in the Rockies, comes into view. That deserves another Caesar.

There's an excellent gourmet meal service and optional activities such as wine-tasting, to put you nicely in the groove of the rocking train. Of course, like many of life's great luxuries, the comfort comes with a price tag. The trip is ideal for Vancouver cruise shippers extending their journey, seniors, or anyone looking for a little bit of romance. Recalling the time I paid ten dollars for an attendant's Snickers bar in Croatia, the only food I had in eighteen hours, I relax knowing that the Rocky Mountaineer is all about the journey, not the destination. If only all journeys were quite as civilized.

START HERE: canadianbucketlist.com/rockymountaineer

SWALLOW A PRAIRIE OYSTER

Chef Aaron Scherr invites me into the restaurant kitchen and pulls out his balls. He asks me if I want to hold them, and I can't deny I'm a little curious. They are grey and slimy, acorn-shaped, with the texture of sponge. They could be the brains of a chipmunk, or perhaps a forgotten, desiccated plum. But no, there's simply no getting around it. These are testicles.

Buzzards Restaurant has had its famous prairie oysters on the menu for two decades, a special addition to the menu during the Calgary Stampede. Now, a cowboy, even one fresh off the ranch, would have to look long and far to find the sea in the Prairies. The fact is, these oysters are as removed from seafood as catnip from a banjo. They do, however, bear some relation to Rocky Mountain Oysters, which you can find south of the border.

A Ballsy Recipe

Chef Aaron Scherr prepares his famous Prairie Oysters:

The Crown Jewels

Ingredients:

1 pair (2) prairie oysters, scrotum removed

2 oz. (60 mL) Crown Royal Canadian rye whisky

3–4 fresh strawberries, quartered or sliced,
   depending on desired presentation

1 4-oz. (125 g) portion of fresh-baked corn bread

1 oz. (30 g) gently crushed walnuts

1 tsp. (5 mL) real maple syrup

1 tbsp. (15 mL) salted butter

salt and pepper—6-to-1 ratio, to taste

Method:

1. Prior to cooking, the oysters (balls) must be blanched and
    cleaned. Bring a pot of salted water to a boil and carefully place
    balls in water. Cook for 3–4 minutes. Remove and place in ice-
    water bath to stop the cooking process. After the testes have
    cooled, carefully remove the external membrane without damag-
    ing the ball. Gently slice into "coins."

2. Preheat a shallow sauté pan over medium temperature, add butter,
    and, as soon as it melts, toss in coins and season with salt and
    pepper. This part of the cooking process is crucial: if the oysters
    get overcooked, they will be rubbery and undesirable, so speed is
    the key to success. Quickly add the strawberries and maple syrup,
    turn up the heat, and hit the pan with Crown. Once the flambé
    subsides, remove from heat and toss with walnuts.

3. On a sexy-lookin' plate, place corn bread slice as the anchor to
    the customer's eye, and cover with contents of pan.

4. Chef's option: Presentation is everything, so feel free to add more
    berries or nuts, a dollop of whipped cream, or a drizzle of heavy
    cream. Serve with ginger beer.

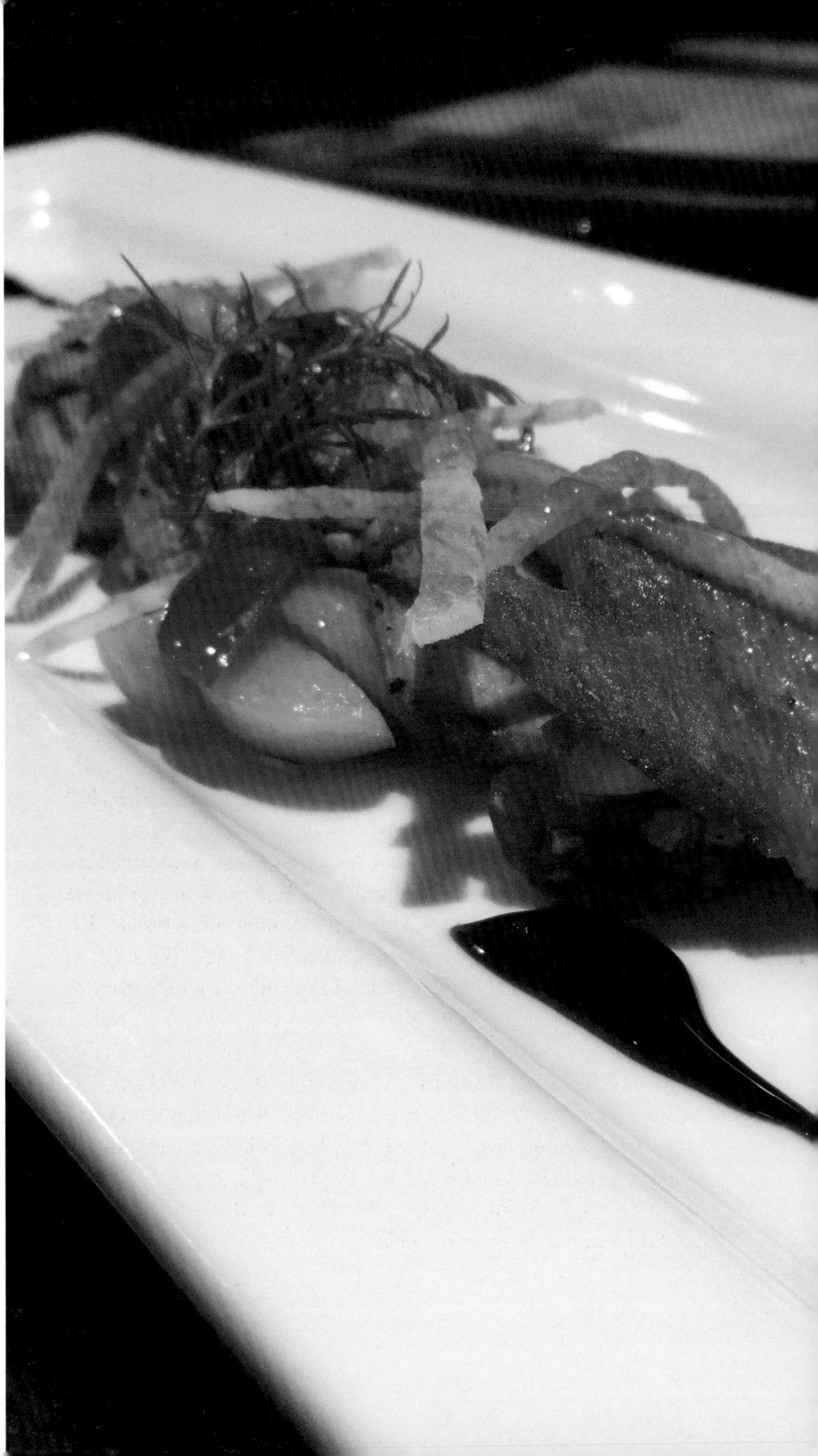

In order for cattle farmers to control their stock, male calves must be castrated. Typically, this is done when they are branded. Alternatively, testicles are tied with elastic, and eventually fall to the ground to be eaten by coyotes (ah, the circle of life!). Some of the balls roll their way to Buzzards, which has thought of several creative ways to cook, grill, and sauté them for the adventurously hungry. Each year they are given a new name and recipe. I was lucky enough to receive the Crown Jewels, to which Scherr adds Crown Royal whisky for flavour.

He hands me a testicle and a sharp knife. I make a cut right at the top and ask him if this makes it kosher. Oh, he's heard them all before, with nigh a sentence passing without a pun. "Sprinkle on nuts, will you?" I ask him if he's lost his marbles. He warns me I might get the sack, and . . . you get the idea.

I slice the organ, rich in protein, into thin, coin-sized medallions. Over the stove, Aaron adds maple butter over high heat, some whisky, salt, fresh-cut strawberries, and gooseberries. For all their novelty on Buzzard's otherwise terrific menu, prairie oysters receive a lot of attention. Buses of Japanese tourists might arrive specifically to sample them. During the ten-day Stampede festival, the chef cooks up over one hundred kilograms of *cajones*.

Lately, sourcing bull balls has become a bit of a problem. Few large meat packers will tackle this soft market, but Aaron has found some farms in his native Saskatchewan to come to the rescue. He even prepared some bison nuts recently, which were bigger than baseballs. Apparently they were a home run with the customers.

He serves up the Crown Jewels at the table. In my travels I have been fortunate to sample crickets (legs get stuck in the teeth), termites (taste nutty), deep-fried guinea pig (stringy chicken), fermented horse milk (acidic), and crocodile (less-stringy chicken). The bucket list demands I eat the testicles of a bull, because this is something to do in Canada. Organ meat tastes like organ meat, and since I grew up on chopped liver, it's not a taste that's unfamiliar to me. Still, I'm not ordering seconds.

I ask for two bottles of beer and pull out my favourite souvenir of all time: a genuine, 100-percent-authentic, hairy kangaroo-scrotum bottle opener, picked up in Australia. The chef thinks I might be yanking his chain, but if you're going to have a themed meal, you might as well go balls to the wall. In the end, culture determines what we find acceptable to consume and what we don't. Eating the gonads of a raging bull, which carry flavour rather well, is deemed unaccept-able by the same society that will happily nosh on pig's feet, liver, rump, and halibut cheeks. The bulls get the snip either way, which keeps coyotes, Japanese tourists, and bucket lists satiated.

START HERE: canadianbucketlist.com/balls

EPILOGUE

My bucket list began with an accident. A car ran a stop sign in downtown Vancouver, plowed into my bike, and broke my kneecap. It was just the sort of brush with death one needs to remind oneself of the importance of living. So I quit my job, cashed in a $20,000 insurance settlement, bought a round-the-world ticket, and set out to tick off my bucket list. Twelve months and twenty-four countries later, I returned home with the realization that bucket lists grow and evolve like the rest of us. Ten years later, I'm still writing new ones. Like a game of whack-a-mole, if you tick one item off at the top, another pops up at the bottom. This proved especially true when I set out to explore the vastness of Canada.

People we meet create the paradise we find, and it is they who shade the colours of our journey. My single biggest piece of advice for any of these experiences: share them with people you like, and if you're on your own, be open and friendly to those around you. Travelling is as personal as the wear and tear on your toothbrush. You might not meet the folks I met, have the same weather, or enjoy each experience as much as I did. How you end up exploring Western Canada will ultimately be as unique as yourself, even if it's only by reading the pages of this book.

While *The Great Western Canada Bucket List* introduced a variety of experiences, I'm well aware there are woeful omissions, items known and less-known that I haven't got to just yet. Visit *canadianbucketlist.com*, and feel free to let me know what they are. I expect this bucket list will keep growing over the years, because the more we dig, the more we'll find, and the more we find, the more we can share with locals and visitors alike.

Grizzly bear viewing, whale watching, hiking with bison, luxury tree houses, one-of-a-kind restaurants and hotels — it seems there's always more to discover. Every chapter in this book concludes with two important words: START HERE. I'll end the book with two more: START NOW.

RE
robin@robinesrock.com
@robinesrock

ACKNOWLEDGEMENTS

This bucket list is the result of many miles and many hours of travel, with the professional and personal help of many people and organizations. My deep gratitude to all below, along with all the airlines, ferries, trains, buses, hotels, B&Bs, and organizations who helped along the way.

BRITISH COLUMBIA: Destination British Columbia, Janice Greenwood-Fraser, Jacqueline Simpson, Andrea Visscher, Lana Kingston, Susan Hubbard, Liz Sperandeo, Teresa Davis, Josie Heisig, Luba Plotnikoff, Geoff Moore (#thanks), Heidi Korven, Cindy Burr, Mika Ryan, Nancie Hall, BC Ferries, Howard Grieve, Morgan Sommerville, Holly Wood, Robin Baycroft, Dee Raffo, Sarah Pearson, Jeremy Roche, CMH guides Rob, Mikey and Bob, heli-ski buddies Natman, David, Dave, Mike, Jim and Larita, Greg McCracken. The WCT crew: Kyle, Jarrod, Robbie, Andrew, Chris and James. Amber Sessions, Jorden Hutchison, Sonu Purhar, Tourism Vancouver. Randy Burke, David Suzuki, Feet Banks, Monica Dickinson, Jeff Topham, Eagle Rider Kamloops, James Nixon, Masa Takei, Doug Firby, Lisa Monforton, Michael Hannan, Rusty Noble, Juliette Recompsat, Jeff and Dianne Pennock, Teneille McGill, Sam Olstead, Graham Bell, Holly Lenk, Katie Dabbs, Lee Newman, T.J. Watt, Bhaskar Krishnamurthy.

ALBERTA: Travel Alberta, Jessica Harcombe-Fleming, Anastasia Martin-Stilwell, Amy Wolski, Hala Dehais, Vanessa Gagnon, Charlie Locke, Tricia Woikin, Mary Morrison, Tessa Mackay, Doug Lentz, ski instructors John Jo and Kaz, Go RVing, Neil English and Isabel, Nancy Dery, Bin Lau, Ralph Sliger, Ian Mackenzie, Ashley Meller.

WORD TRAVELS CAST AND CREW: Sean Cable, Neil MacLean, Zach Williams, Heather Hawthorne-Doyle, Julia Dimon, Leah Kimura, Caroline Manuel, Deb Wainwright, Mike Bodnarchuk, Peter Steel, Paul Vance, Patrice Baillargeon.

SPECIAL THANKS: David Rock, Karen McMullin, Margaret Bryant, Kirk Howard, Carrie Gleason, Allison Hirst, Synora van Drine, Courtney Horner, Hilary McMahon, Cathy Hirst, Jon Rothbart, Elyse Mailhot, Ian Mackenzie, Sean Aiken, Gary Kalmek, Joe Kalmek, Heather Taylor, Guy Theriault, Jennifer Burnell, Lauren More, Joshua Norton, Ann Campbell, Linda Bates, Patrick Crean, Gloria Loree, Ernst Flach, the Canadian Tourism Commission and all at Go Media Marketplace, Josephine Wasch, Ken Hegan, Jarrod Levitan, Vancouver and Burnaby Public Libraries, Zebunnisa Mirza, Sherill Sirrs, Chris Lee, Marc Telio, Brandon Furyk, Mary Rostad, RtCamp, and the Kalmek and Esrock families.

SPECIAL THANKS TO THE FOLLOWING, WITHOUT WHOM THERE WOULD BE NO COMPANION WEBSITE OR SPEAKING TOURS: Ford Canada, Parks Canada, VIA Rail, Travel Manitoba, Tourism Saskatchewan, Tourism New Brunswick, Destination BC, Tourism Prince Edward Island, World Expeditions, and Keen Footwear.

And finally, thank you to my parents, Joe and Cheryl Kalmek (without whom there would be no Robin Esrock), my ever-supportive wife, Ana Carolina, and my daughter, Raquel: *Yay! Aipane! Uppee!*

PHOTO CREDITS

74 Jeff Topham
76 Jeff Topham

SPOT THIS SPOTTED LAKE
75 Robin Esrock

LET IT HANG OUT ON WRECK
BEACH
77 Robin Escrock
78 Guilhem Vellut, https://
flic.kr/p/9BoLTs.
Licence at http://
creativecommons.org/
licenses/by/2.0.

CLIMB A MOUNTAIN WITH NO
EXPERIENCE
80 Courtesy CMH Summer
Adventures
81 Courtesy CMH Summer
Adventures

FLOAT THE PENTICTON RIVER
CHANNEL
82 Melissa Barnes/Penticton
& Wine Country
Tourism
83 Kyle Pearce, https://flic.
kr/p/4WrVif. Licence at
http://creativecommons.
org/licenses/by/2.0.
84 Robin Esrock
85 Robin Esrock

CLIMB THE GRIND, HIKE THE
CHIEF
86 Robin Esrock
87 Robin Esrock
88 Robin Esrock

SEA TO SKY GONDOLA
89 Courtesy Sea to Sky
Gondola/Paul Bride
89 Courtesy Sea to Sky
Gondola/Paul Bride

EXPERIENCE THE CALGARY
STAMPEDE
92 Robin Esrock

94 Robin Esrock
94 Ian Mackenzie
95 Ian Mackenzie

SKI IN A UNESCO WORLD
HERITAGE SITE
96 Banff Lake Louise
Tourism/Paul Zizka
Photography
97 Banff Lake Louise
Tourism/Paul Zizka
Photography
99 Banff Lake Louise
Tourism/Paul Zizka
Photography

HUNT FOR DINOSAURS
100 Robin Esrock
101 Robin Esrock
102 Robin Esrock

HELI-YOGA IN THE ROCKIES
104 Robin Esrock
105 Robin Esrock
105 Robin Esrock
107 Robin Esrock

HIKE THE SKY
108 DSC_0172 by Michael
Lawton, https://flic.
kr/p/6LLBdt. Licence at
http://creativecommons.
org/licenses/by/2.0.

BE THE COWBOY ON A RANCH
VACATION
110 Robin Esrock
111 Robin Esrock
112–13 Robin Esrock
114 Robin Esrock

RV THE ICEFIELDS PARKWAY
116 Gary Kalmek
118 Gary Kalmek
119 Gary Kalmek

CANOE ON MORAINE LAKE
120 Moraine Lake Lodge
121 Moraine Lake Lodge

STEP OVER THE ROCKIES
122 Courtesy Brewster Travel
123 Courtesy Brewster Travel
124 Robin Esrock
125 Robin Esrock

VISIT AN OASIS OF WILDLIFE
126 Bison by Michelle Tribe,
https://flic.kr/p/72V8nH.
Licence at http://
creativecommons.org/
licenses/by/2.0.

HIT YOUR TARGET AT THE WEST
EDMONTON MALL
128 Courtesy of West
Edmonton Mall and
Edmonton Economic
Development
Corporation

HIKE OR SKI INTO SKOKI LODGE
131 Robin Esrock
133 Robin Esrock
133 Robin Esrock
134 Robin Esrock

VISIT A SITE FOR ALL EYES
135 Courtesy Tourism Jasper
136 Courtesy Tourism Jasper

BOARD THE ROCKY MOUNTAINEER
138 Courtesy Rocky
Mountaineer
139 Courtesy Rocky
Mountaineer
140 Courtesy Rocky
Mountaineer
140 Courtesy Rocky
Mountaineer

SWALLOW A PRAIRIE OYSTER
142 Ian Mackenzie
144 Courtesy Buzzards Bar
and Restaurant

🏛 DUNDURN

VISIT US AT
Dundurn.com
@dundurnpress
Facebook.com/dundurnpress
Pinterest.com/dundurnpress